T0244115

In my lifetime two British trainers have been blessed with a touch of genius: Sir Henry Cecil and Nicky Henderson. This book – via tales about his brilliant horses – takes you on a roller-coaster ride with Nicky's triumphs and tragedies, heady racedays and disasters, plus gives you a unique insight in to the mind of that training genius.

Ed Chamberlin,
ITV Racing

A beautiful portrait of the love between Nicky Henderson and his greatest horses. Intimate, revealing and unforgettable, with a long reach in racing but also far beyond.

Paul Hayward,
five times Sports Writer of the Year

Nicky Henderson's career is a timeless masterpiece, with craft and thought put into every horse. The attention to detail in this beautiful book is similarly meticulous. A must read.

Dominic King,
Racing Correspondent, *The Daily Mail*

A brilliant and original portrait of a man with an exceptional gift. Where others see horses, Nicky Henderson sees magic, sophistication and complex personalities – he's like the Shakespeare of racing.

Ed Needham,
Strong Words magazine

This is a book every racing fan should read. For it takes a fresh look at famous horses and jumping's most famous trainer. In the very best of senses, it puts new wine in old bottles.

Brough Scott MBE, racing journalist,
broadcaster, author and former jockey

A brilliant insight into the life, knowledge, passion and intuition that Nicky has, and gives his horses on a daily basis. All of which makes him one of the greatest trainers and horsemen of any generation, and above all an absolute gentleman.

Barry Geraghty, first stable jockey to
Nicky Henderson from 2008-2015

A full, personable and bewitching account of the genius that is the six-time champion jumps trainer – while this is a must-read for racing fans, I'd recommend it to anyone who has ever loved an animal.

Martha Terry, *Horse & Hound*

NICKY HENDERSON

My Life in 12 Horses

with
Kate Johnson

First published by Pitch Publishing, 2023
Reprinted, 2023
3

Pitch Publishing
9 Donnington Park,
85 Birdham Road,
Chichester,
West Sussex,
PO20 7AJ
www.pitchpublishing.co.uk
info@pitchpublishing.co.uk

A CIP catalogue record is available for this book
from the British Library.

ISBN 978 1 80150 490 4

Typesetting and origination by Pitch Publishing
Printed and bound in Great Britain by TJ Books, Padstow

CONTENTS

For my family; Mum,

Philip, Ed and

Stop the Show

ACKNOWLEDGEMENTS

I'M SO grateful that Nicky Henderson LVO OBE said yes to this idea. He was unfailingly generous, available (he once offered to telephone on his only free day, which was Christmas Day), and fascinating. Thank you, and to Sophie, who was always so kind, and to Bronwyn and Marie in the office.

Sincere thanks to everyone who made time to talk to me; the legendary Corky Browne and his wife Diane, bloodstock agent David Minton, National Hunt trainers Charlie Mann, Richard Phillips and Oliver Sherwood, and Irish trainer Ian Ferguson. And the proud owners; Ronnie Bartlett, Michael Buckley, Jenny Collins, Malcolm Kimmins, Caroline Mould, Piers Pottinger, Josie Reed and Robert Waley-Cohen. I'm lost in admiration for jockeys Eddie Ahern, Bob Davies, Nico de Boinville, Richard Dunwoody, Mick Fitzgerald, John Francome, Barry Geraghty, Richard Johnson OBE, Sir AP McCoy OBE, Jamie Osborne, Steve Smith-Eccles, Andrew Tinkler and Sam Waley-Cohen, and moved by the devotion of yard staff Dave Fehily, Caroline Gordon, Lara Hegarty, Chris Jerdin, Jake Loader, Iain Major, Sarwar Mohammed, James Nixon, Aaron Rid, Sarah Shreeve and Helen Stevens.

Aintree's cheerleaders, Charles Barnett, former managing director of Aintree Racecourse, Lord Daresbury, the former chairman and Jane Clarke, Grand National historian and Aintree tour guide filled me in on the history. Paddy Behan, Lois Eadie, and Sally Noott and Ciara Carty reminisced about the foals that turned into superstars.

Professor Linda Keeling, Dr Leanne Proops and Associate Professor Dr Jane Williams freely shared their intriguing research. Sports psychologist Michael Caulfield, RCVS recognised veterinary specialists Kate Allen and Celia Marr, veterinary equine behaviourist Gemma Pearson, and senior racecourse veterinary surgeons Lesley Barwise-Munro and Simon Knapp took the time to explain hugely complicated things in simple language.

The former boss of the Retraining Of Racehorses charity Di Arbuthnot, the sculptor Philip Blacker, the commentators Richard Hoiles and Simon Holt, Punchestown racing manager Richie Galway, Debbie Matthews, Miranda Murton, Vicky Roberts, presenter Alice Plunkett, and caretaker to the stars Tracy Vigors shared their stories.

Thanks to Jane Camillin at Pitch Publishing for her great support, Katie Field, Michelle Grainger and now Paul Hayward at Racing Post Books, I am so glad to have benefitted from their experience, expertise and enthusiasm.

Final thanks to the horses, for being magnificent.

INTRODUCTION BY
MICHAEL BUCKLEY

HORSE RACING had become a big part of my life by the early 1980s, and I seemed to be on an endless round of race meetings, parties, and lunches with people involved in the sport. I had met a lot of 'larger than life' and amusing people who were involved in horses, well known characters such as Robert Sangster, John Magnier, JP McManus, Jeremy Hindley, Charles Benson, Billy McDonald and many other extraordinary folk who inhabited that world. I had bought horses from various trainers and traders in Ireland, and yearlings at the English sales, and my life became a juggling act of finding enough money and time to support owning horses with regular visits to Cheltenham, Royal Ascot, Newmarket, Newbury, and anywhere else that was fun and full of people from the world of horse racing!

It was a life somewhat divorced from reality, but owning horses is based on dreams which most frequently are very far from reality.

It was at that time that Nicky Henderson fortuitously came into my life. A slim, bright, blue-eyed young man in the early stages of what was to become an illustrious career predominantly training National Hunt racehorses.

I bought my first horse in 1974, who won a race, and I was hooked for all time. Thinking this must be an easy game, I bought more horses which I could ill afford, and I was incredibly lucky winning many races including the Hennessy Gold Cup and the Whitbread Gold Cup within three years of starting out as an owner. I even bought half of Grand Canyon over lunch, who went on to win the Colonial Cup in South Carolina, which paid for me to go to Las Vegas and see Elvis Presley perform. And it was my first visit to America! Racing horses was the best fun, so easy to enjoy, and seemed to be rewarding in every way.

Inevitably I came down to earth with a bang. With numerous fallers, injuries and disappointments, I had soon experienced the full highs and lows of being a National Hunt owner.

By the time I met Nicky, my original trainer had retired, as had all the good horses I had owned. Business was tough, but I needed to start again, and it seemed that this talented and fun young trainer was also a sympathetic person with whom I could enjoy the good days and deal with the bad ones.

We have had horses together for close to 40 years, and whilst plenty have been quite moderate we have also been lucky enough to enjoy some extraordinarily talented athletes. There have been celebrations and laughs all along the way, interspersed with tears of joy and some of very deep sadness. Some of the most fun but frustrating days were spent on a number of skiing holidays we had together, when we found out that our skiing skills didn't quite match our talent for having fun later in the evening!

I have been told several times that I can be quite tricky or difficult, and yet Nicky and I seem to have had few if any disagreements during our long association and friendship. This says a lot for Nick's enduring patience with humans as well as his renowned patience with horses.

As you read this book, you will get to see the care and individual flair which Nicky brings to training each horse. It always amazes me how different horses are, how they each require individual methods of training, and yet each one is prepared with the same objective of covering a particular distance faster than the opposition.

As the world knows, this man is a master trainer who frequently refers to a particular horse as being 'a very nice person'. That expression exemplifies his gift for treating each horse according to its characteristics.

I can assure every reader of this book that Nicky is also a very nice person, a man of rare patience and good humour, and these qualities are reflected in the relaxed way in which horses from Seven Barrows continue to be competitive year after year.

And now we are joined together in living a most unlikely dream, which is the reality of having Constitution Hill in our lives. Whilst the thought of being around a horse as good as 'The Hill' seems thrilling, the reality of owning him is indescribable and so much better. I am so lucky to have him, that he came from Barry Geraghty who is a dear friend, is ridden by Nico de Boinville who is such an accomplished and cool horseman, and trained by the incomparable Nicky Henderson.

I admire him and love him. As you would, too.

1

HAPPY WARRIOR

The willing, winning grey that started it all

'HE RAN away with me completely. I was going further and further clear, I couldn't hold him, and finally we turned into the straight and I heard from behind me jockeys screaming "GET OUT OF THE WAY YOU AMATEUR!"' says Nicky Henderson LVO OBE, fondly.

It was just his second ever spin on Happy Warrior, a colossal and obliging five-year-old grey, given to Nicky by his parents for his 21st birthday, as what may be the world's most glamorous present. He was an actual amateur jockey, so the chorus from the pros behind him on this two-and-a-half-mile hurdle race at Kempton wasn't necessarily as insulting as it sounds, and anyway, being yelled at brought him nothing but relief. He was exhausted from being carted around by a horse who raced with genuine enthusiasm, and he couldn't wait to pull up.

So, 'I got out of the way' he remembers, 'waved them by, and let them all go up my inside. Which obviously you should never do.' Five thundered past; just the sharpener the Warrior needed, and Nicky reappeared upsides at the last, in his white silks with dark blue hoops, charged to the front and hurtled past the post. Victory! On 16 November 1972, aged 22, his first winner logged and date-stamped into his DNA, with his delighted family watching on.

That's Nicky's version, 50 years on, that he somehow won despite having no control and no clue, hanging on to his beloved berserker. Of course, nobody, but nobody, has ever won a race by incompetence or chance in a sport so uniquely and seriously dangerous that ambulances follow every iteration and where jockeys are so close to each other they can talk without shouting and bang stirrups. Nobody races to come second. A dangerous jockey is a death-wish jockey, and unlikely to get a second spin, even on their own mount, and Nicky is and always was a horseman to his bones; skilful, natural, instinctive as well as a competitive, serious, responsible, amateur jockey.

After his debut at Newbury, his mother had turned to her friend Fred Winter, the esteemed Lambourn trainer where the Warrior was housed and from where Nicky rode out. Bursting with pride, she beamed, 'Didn't he do well!' Fred replied grimly, 'He'll have to do a bloody sight better than that.' And he did, exactly that, in his very next race.

In those days, he'd ride out first thing in the morning for Fred in Lambourn, hotfoot it to London to put in a shift at the stockbroking and investment bank Cazenove, following in his father's distinguished footsteps, then saddle up and race at weekends when he could. He won his next at Towcester too, and the intrepid duo's next stop was Cheltenham. Nicky maintains, 'I rode him appallingly. I went round the world, over Cleeve Hill, round the back of the stands. Fred was fuming. I should have won.' Fred was the pro and Nicky was the amateur and they both wanted to win races but the problem was, it all happened so fast. 'You're at the start, then you're off and if you're not on the ball you get left behind. It took about four goes to find that it's rather easy to get left.'

The falls aren't softer for amateurs, dehydration is no less depleting, and Nicky handled it all, the injuries ('not for the first time I ended up at Cheltenham General Hospital…'), and making the weight (he weighed 9st 7lb, riding at 9st 12lb, but he was living alone, 'cooking' for himself and a single boiled egg was the only dish on the menu), being permanently dehydrated, spending hours sitting in the local sauna every night, and guzzling 'pee pills' (pill poppers were easy to spot, taken desperately short and having to hop off their horses on returning from the gallops).

Just weeks after that first win, fate sent its wrecking ball, obliterating the familiar landscape and the loving springboard into life, and leaving an indelible line, between what had gone before and what would come after.

* * *

Nicky's adored mother, Katherine Sarah Beckwith-Smith (always known as Sarah) was a natural and accomplished horsewoman. She loved horses, rode beautifully and was joint-master of the Craven Hounds. Nicky recalls one Boxing Day meet at Newbury, which always brought throngs of people to line the main street and watch the hounds. After gathering in the market place, the hunt would set off clattering down the road, led by the master. Always led by the master, it was as infra dig as passing the port to the right to overtake and anyone getting ahead could be sent home in mortifying disgrace. Nicky's pony had no truck with such twee etiquette; ponies have a strong sense of self (the classic small person syndrome balanced on four tiny hooves), often refusing to do what they know full well they are being asked to do, trit-trotting jauntily out of a show ring having flatly refused three times at the first fence. They're also the best partners in crime a child could wish for, inspiring a first love that may never be bettered and leaving them a bit braver than they found them. As the hunt moved, this one chose freedom, over the bridge, the pelican crossing, steaming past the clock tower, and of course, the masters, at least one of whom found it highly amusing.

* * *

Years later, hundreds of happy miles ridden, Sarah suffered a terrible accident. Nicky says simply, 'She was riding down a road, and she slipped over and banged her head.'

When he recalls it, his natural ebullience temporarily deserts him, his forensic memory too. The needle skids off the record and the music stops. He can't remember who telephoned him in London to tell him the desperate news, or the words they used. He gathered with his brother, sister and father at the John Radcliffe hospital in Oxford, where they stayed with family friends for two days. His mother died in hospital aged 46.

'Everybody adored her,' Nicky says, 'she was great fun, she loved life like nobody else. It was party time! She was great, everybody would say she was a very special person. My brother and sister and I have been very lucky and privileged.'

He remembers the idyllic childhood, summers in Scotland learning to fish (he didn't have a passport until he was 19), careening on ponies, the close family ties. Sister Josie agrees, 'It was blissful, we adored each other and we did all the riding together. Nicky was a gorgeous older brother, such a kind person, we were always very good friends.'

* * *

The days after Sarah's death were dark, the siblings too distressed to see that their father Johnny was suffering, 'He lost what he loved too. It was a tough time,' Nicky says now. Josie, then a teen, says, 'It was a terrible time, we were all devastated. It's a difficult subject, we all got through it as best we could. To be honest, 50 years later it's still a trauma. It was so unexpected … no chance to say goodbye and it wasn't just us who were devastated. I still see people who remember when it happened and my dad was knocked sideways by it as well.'

After a while, Nicky returned to riding out in the mornings, and banking in the day, feeling 'a lot happier around horses than behind a desk'. There's a lot behind such a simple phrase. As the saying goes, there's something about the outside of a horse that is good for the inside of a man. Balancing motionless over the spine of a half-tonne animal with no brakes is all-consuming exercise, and the effort releases feel-good endorphins. Racehorses are walking works of art, even grooming can produce increased levels of serotonin (a mood-boosting chemical that the body produces naturally), and decreased stress levels.

Horses literally know how you're feeling. Dr Leanne Proops from the University of Portsmouth led a study in which horses were shown a photo of either an angry or happy face and then met either the same person or a different person many hours later. The horses that had seen the angry faces showed signs of stress like self-scratching, and looked with their left eye (which goes to the right side of the brain, which deals with threats) when they saw that same person later, but the horses that had seen happy faces or a completely different person, didn't.

Dr Proops describes this as a 'memory for emotion' and says, 'There are some things you feel pretty sure horses can do but this study was able to demonstrate the ability scientifically. If you think about it, there are a lot of complex things that are required: they need to be able to recognise human facial expressions – no easy feat – and they need to individually recognise the person, transfer that recognition from a photo to the real person, and they need to remember both the identity and the emotion for several hours.' It's not just supremely intelligent, she adds, 'It's magical too; they're amazing.'

After an ending, there must be a beginning. Nicky knew he couldn't spend his life at Cazenove. He was adrift, in need of someone to see that they were all in 'a bit of a muddle' and to offer a light through the darkness. That someone was Fred Winter.

'What are you doing?' Fred asked, without inviting an answer. 'You're not enjoying that. Why don't you come and work for me, I need an assistant.'

Nicky replied, 'Can you go and talk to father please, and ask him if I can?' He was expected to follow his dad's career, stay at Cazenove, and take on the family estate too as the first-born son. Fred duly approached Johnny and Nicky was of course released.

'Fred was the hand that came out to rescue me,' he says. 'The whole Winter family became like brothers and sisters, like my family for a couple of years.' He adds, 'He was tough too, it wasn't out of complete sympathy: you're going to work.'

* * *

Work he did; riding out three lots every morning, and learning his craft in the most stellar company. The best horses were housed in 'millionaires' row', with household names like Bula, Crisp, Pendil, and Lanzarote, though Fred's favourites that he adored and rode every day were the violent rogues. 'He fell in love with some very odd characters, moody, moderate horses who went to the races and didn't try – the rascals, brilliant in the morning, absolute monkeys in the afternoon. Fred loved them because he could win every gallop on them. He loved being competitive.'

He was the best trainer, locked in mortal combat with trainer Fulke Walwyn 'over the wall' next door, intense rivals and the best of friends. 'I probably learned as much from head lad Brian Delaney as I did from Fred. He did all the feeding, did the legs, he was in charge of all the problems.'

The riders weren't bad either; none other than John Francome pitched up as a 16-year-old leading showjumper and made everyone else feel like clowns with his perfect balance, like a self-levelling table on an ocean liner. Charlie Mann, a stable jockey at the time, later a trainer, says, 'He didn't move, he just squeezed the horse.' Fred's magpie eye saw it straight away. Nicky says, John 'changed race riding completely. He could see strides – eight strides from a fence – and he could present a horse at a fence: 3-2-1. Jockeys used to ride horses at a fence with very little finesse. There were odd horses he couldn't get on with who wouldn't listen if they didn't like being told what to do, or couldn't understand what he was trying to do, but he was totally unique and fantastic to watch.'

Up until a few years ago, John still rode out for Nicky. 'I'd say, "Do you want to school?" He'd say, "Yes," and I'd get all the kids here and say, "Come and watch this, it's as good as you'll ever see." You can't teach someone to be a good jockey, or, rather, you can only teach so much. AP McCoy and John Francome are 90 per cent natural talent, and the first 75 is hand-eye coordination.'

John plays it down, 'I was in the right place at the right time. I never wanted to be a jockey, I never sat on the back of a chair thinking I was going to be Lester Piggott. I wanted to earn a good living and ride nice horses; it wasn't the be-all and end-all, but I'd spent every hour of the day riding and I knew I could do it. With riding, something clicks, or it doesn't.' He tells any young jockeys asking for advice that, 'The horse is doing 99 per cent of the work, you ought to spend more time thinking about what the horse is doing than what you're doing. If you give someone a piggy back, it's ten times easier to carry them if they sit still than if they're jumping all over the place.'

John is immensely engaging and wears his natural horsemanship so lightly that when he says, 'I could do anything,' he means he'd service Fred's car, ferry his children to school, and put in a staircase up to the loft. He admits, 'Jumping was never a problem for me. Part of it was seeing a stride, understanding what Fred wanted and what I wanted. You can't teach a horse to jump going too fast. It's a simple thing: you go to the schooling ground, and the way you turn them in to the jump, the first hurdle, it's important how they set off. Whoever wants to be on the outside, wheel round the inside horse, make sure the stick's in the other hand, the one that's a bit green [inexperienced] goes in the middle. It's got to be enjoyable for them and that's what I brought to it.'

To this day, Nicky applies the methods and techniques he learned as Fred's assistant. It's often simple stuff. 'I ask every single rider every single morning, "All OK? All happy?" before we set off and when they come back. Knowing your horses is the most important thing.' John agrees, saying, 'A good lad on a horse he rides every day, should be able to say after going ten yards, this horse doesn't feel right. Some can drive down the road and not know the door's not shut or the window's open; some haven't got out the garage and they know.'

The specifics of Fred's routines wouldn't work today. On Mondays, they'd walk through Lambourn. The sign at the outskirts says, 'Valley of the racehorse' but in those days it was their kingdom too and the realm's benign leaders would trot out to the next village, Eastbury, up the hill, walk down it, trot home. They'd be out for an hour trotting on the roads, 20 horses in two groups of ten always in single file and every Tuesday they'd go to the gallops.

'The art is to trot very slowly – now they all trot too fast – up hill as slow as you can go as it makes them work harder,' Nicky explains. 'There'd be a gap in the middle of the string so cars could pass the first ten and slot in, then the lad at the back would shout "car behind", and the lad at the front would shout "hold it" or "wave him on". All the cars did exactly as they were told, we controlled the traffic, we were respectful with people trying to get to work or school but Lambourn was all about horses. If I told someone here we did that twice a week, they'd think you'd lost the plot, they'd laugh and say "You can't do that". We only cantered twice a week that's why the lads all got run away with, the horses were so fresh.'

All-weather gallops, infra-red heat lamps, on-site physiotherapists, water treadmills, and heart-rate monitors didn't exist. 'Do we go faster now? No. But we know a lot more now than we did then,' Nicky says. 'We never found out why a horse was lame, because we couldn't scan, and couldn't x-ray, scoping was unheard of. If a horse went lame, we shut it in its box until it was sound, there was nothing you could do. We used to think everything was lame in the shoulder, in fact we very seldom get shoulder injuries, it's almost certainly in the knee, we had no way of finding out.' Accidents and injury time are minimised now, though even with all the science in the world, 'you won't believe what a horse can do, put one in a padded cell and something will go wrong'.

* * *

Come 1977, the increasingly aptly named Happy Warrior was still going strong. That year, he lined up with Nicky for the Fox Hunters' Chase at Aintree; every amateur's dream, in what would be an historic year for the meeting.

Peter O'Sullevan captured the last seconds of the most exciting ten minutes of live sport in the world as Red Rum, ridden by Tommy Stack, took his third Grand National with the words, 'He's coming up to the line to win it like a fresh horse in great style. It's hats off and a tremendous reception, you've never heard one like it at Liverpool! Red Rum wins the National!' The horse pricked his ears as he passed the post, ecstatic crowds, quite insanely, ran on to the turf to greet him and he was serenaded with 'For He's a Jolly Good Fellow' in the winner's enclosure.

The bay in the sheepskin noseband attended the ceremony to collect his BBC Sports Personality of the Year award, became the most fleet-of-foot national treasure, is still the most famous horse in Britain, and is credited with renewing the popularity of Aintree, which was under threat from property developers. When Red Rum died aged 30 in 1995 (he is buried at the winning post at Aintree), someone suggested to his trainer Ginger McCain that it must have felt like losing a wife. 'There's 25 million women in this country,' he replied, 'and if I lose the wife, I could certainly get another woman. But I could never get another Red Rum. He was a one-off.'

The crowds were smaller in those days, about 8,000 compared to 70,000 now, but the fences were bigger. You could drive a Mini through the 6ft wide open ditch in front of the 5ft 2in thorn fence of the Chair (one of three fences with a gaping ditch in front). Becher's and Valentine's Brook both had a natural brook 5ft 6in wide on the landing side, so deep it had gates at the end as there was no other way to get a horse out should it end up in there.

Nicky and the Warrior would be jumping all the same fences as Red Rum, one circuit instead of two. Also riding that day was Peter Greenall (now Lord Daresbury). He went on to become chairman of Aintree in 1988 and was responsible for changing the fortunes of the racecourse. First, with the fences, 'We felt we wanted to have public opinion behind Aintree. The statistics were stark, 50 per cent of Grand National racers over a 20-year period fell on the way to Becher's the first time, and that isn't a good experience.' And then improving the experience from the slightly 'shabby' days of the 1980s, bringing in a classy sponsor (Martell), and bumping up the prize money from £180,000 to £1 million.

Back in 1977, Peter was riding Timmie's Battle, and the decades have not dimmed his pleasure in riding a winner as he remembers, 'I rode in the Fox Hunters' seven times and finally won in 1982; it took me a bit of time, on Lone Soldier, at 33/1. JM Wilson rode for Fred Winter and was hot favourite and I beat him.' In the weighing room, he remembers, 'On the big days, the noisy ones were quiet and the quiet ones were noisy. It was a big stage; it's not Ludlow.'

Robert Waley-Cohen was another taking part, and went on to became the chairman of Cheltenham, as well as a hugely successful owner. He remembers getting changed in the old weighing room – now a bar – and feeling the 'ghosts of the nineteenth century heroes, it was an astonishing atmosphere'. He also recalls cantering to the start thinking, 'What on earth am I doing here? I'm completely out of my class. I must be mad.'

Luckily, it passed. 'I felt a great deal better when I got down there and Joey Newton's horse wouldn't stop so he aimed it at the wooden rails. It jumped over, off the racecourse then wouldn't jump back on again. The start was delayed while they sent for an axe to cut down the rail.' He thought, 'I'm going to make a complete fool of myself but hopefully not like that.'

It was a grey, drizzly day and the loud speaker system had conked out. 'Somebody had a fall at the Chair and lay on their back staring at the sky while the ambulances drove past him,' Robert says, 'My wife was heavily pregnant in the stands, and worried that if I fell off at the furthest end of the course, no one would know and they'd never find me.'

Like any sportsperson, he remembers this most daunting of races as though it were yesterday. His worries that he was out of his depth were unfounded. 'We got to the Canal Turn and we went so tight we gained quite a lot of ground and went from not being anywhere to fourth. We hit a perfect stride at Valentine's and sailed over it. It's the nearest thing you can get to flying on a horse; properly big fences, enormous drops … you're in the air for an awfully long time.'

The romance of Valentine's was lost on Nicky. 'At that point I realised for some reason, his neck was getting longer and longer. The saddle had started to go backwards and backwards, I thought I was going to run out of rein and I was sat on his backside.' It got worse, the girth now working its way to the Warrior's rear end, and as they came round the bend to the straight, the saddle began slipping to one side. Nicky was throwing his weight the other way to get it back in the middle where it belonged. All of this at a racing gallop in a field of half-tonne horses trying to barrel past him.

As he was attempting to throw the saddle over, he slammed into Rusty Tears (his jockey later objected but was overruled) and somehow he survived the last two fences before he claimed victory. It was a courageous, exceptionally adept ride and a tremendous win. Back in the winner's enclosure, Fred had one question, 'Why did you let him up your inside?' 'I didn't have a saddle,' Nicky answered.

The Warrior hadn't worn a breast girth. When kit was being assigned the night before, it was decided he didn't need one but the fences had upright stakes made of birch which would catch their girths, and the size of the fences meant the horse had to reach more.

'I've never sent a horse out since without a breast girth. Every single horse I run wears a white one since that day,' Nicky says of the distinctive look that gives his horses the air of breasting the tape in an old fashioned 100yd dash.

The other lesson Nicky learned from that day is how surprisingly friendless it feels to be at the start of the Grand National course. 'It's the loneliest place you'll ever be, walking round and round in endless circles on your horse that can't talk to you. You look at the stands and there are a million people looking at you, on televisions round the world, people are looking at you, all talking and giggling and there's just 40 of you walking round.

'It's the only time you'll see jockeys quiet in the weighing room before the race, it isn't the usual banter. You know it's different. You get to the start, and it's quiet, you can't hear anything, but you know. You're sat on your own, you're all thinking it's about to start, it'll be cut-throat and flat out and it's a very lonely place for five minutes.'

So, whenever he's had a National runner, he goes to the start with them, walks round with his jockey, checks the girth, chats, waves them off with a 'go out and enjoy yourselves' and then dashes to a vantage point.

* * *

It's no surprise that Fred wasn't sympathetic when Nicky was in danger of disappearing out the side door of the Warrior. No horseman knows all there is to know about these enigmatic equine athletes, but Fred must have come close. He'd been champion jockey four times, winning the races that every jockey dreams of – two Grand Nationals, two Gold Cups, three Champion Hurdles. And they weren't even his greatest achievements as a jockey; at the 1962 Grand Steeple Chase de Paris in Auteuil he partnered Fulke Walwyn's horse, Mandarin. He was weak, from starving himself to make the weight, the horse was ridden in a rubber-covered steel bit, and it snapped in his mouth at the fourth of 30 fences around a four-mile figure of eight course. If he'd been driving, it would have been like the brake cable snapping, the steering wheel coming loose in his hands and the accelerator pedal jamming on, all in three lanes of traffic. In a feat of supreme prowess, and the uplifting superhuman nobility that only reveals itself in rare sporting moments, they stayed the course, they won the race. And the one after.

Fred turned to training after riding, when the Jockey Club bafflingly rejected him for a starter's job. He was champion eight times. He won the Grand National with his first two runners in the race. He was firm, fair, brilliant and true, a man by whom jockeys and trainers will be forever measured. His eye was remarkable, his methods still used by his former protégés today, who learned by looking. Fred didn't go in for explanations and so much about horses can't be taught or even put into words.

Nicky and John Francome knew better than to talk to him before 10am and in John's 15 years with Fred, ('a wonderful loyal person'), he never made it as far as his kitchen. He usually drove him to the races four days a week, when he'd be 'lucky to get six words'. At the end of the meeting, he'd change out of his silks, drive home, never stop on the way, never go into the house for a drink. Years later, John was startled to discover there were bars at racecourses. He says, 'You were taught to do it properly, he trained how he wanted. If at the end of the year, he'd made money, that was good, if he hadn't, not the end of the world, there was never a question that we weren't going to steam clean the boxes or clean the tack or the rugs at the end of the season, or have the best food and hay. It would be impossible to go and work for anyone else.'

The attention to detail was a searchlight that could see round corners; Albert Browne (known by all except Fred as Corky as he came from Cork) worked in the yard and remembers walking home one day with a bunch of daffodils. Fred appeared upsides in his car. 'Can I give you a lift, Albert?' 'No thanks.' 'Come on, those flowers look heavy. I've got some just like them, same colour.' 'Is that right?' 'Yes, in my garden, who are they for?' 'My wife, Diane.' 'I hope she enjoys them.'

* * *

To ride at any level is to accept risk, though some might be startled that what happened to Nicky's mother didn't put him off horses. 'It certainly didn't,' he says, 'When I came right, I decided I was going to give this a go, and Dad was fantastic, and gave me the opportunity to do it. He may have thought, this won't last long, and is going to cost a few quid, we'll soon find out. In fact, I wouldn't be surprised if he thought, what on earth are you doing?'

Johnny died aged 83, and for years after, Nicky would think, what do I do about this and that? I know! I'll ring up the old man and see-what-he-thinks-oh-no-I-can't. Having been denied the chance of an adult relationship with his mother, there must have been hundreds of times too when he thought, I'd love to talk to mum about this horse? 'Oh, not just about horses,' he says, 'about anything.'

When Nicky was established as a trainer, Johnny used to write to him after a big race and say, 'wouldn't Mum be proud'. 'That's why it's important she saw me ride my first winner,' he says. wedssscx34 'She'd seen the start, but she never saw this end, and she would have loved it. I hope Dad was proud, I think he was. Nobody knew it was going to finish up like this. I suppose I always assumed I'd be a stockbroker who had a few rides.'

After five years as assistant trainer, he ended his jockey career with 75 wins, including the Imperial Cup on Fred's Acquaint, and five hunter chases on Rolls Rambler, which culminated in the Horse and Hound Cup Final Champion Hunters' Chase at Stratford on 3 June 1978, his last ride.

It was time for Nicky to move on, Fred knew it too, and told him to find his replacement.

* * *

Oliver Sherwood heard the best assistant trainer's job in the country might be up for grabs and wrote to Fred and Nicky. Nicky's letter back was encouraging, with the joke-but-not-really that he'd need to bring a very good horse with him. His father's Venture to Cognac would do. Later he added a second condition; if he got the job, he'd have to buy Nicky's house, Frisky's Place (named after the previous owner, truly).

When Oliver came for his trial, the Gold Cup, postponed to April due to snow, was won by John Francome on Fred's Midnight Court. It must have felt like the time was right and the stars were aligned. They weren't. Oliver's host, Nicky, had broken his collarbone. Painful, to mortals, yet a jockey's first thought is not the pain, but how long they'll be off for. Oliver was pressed into service. 'I remember being woken up a couple of times in the night by his screams for help. He got cast in his bed and I had to go and rescue him.' Frustrated by 'medical' advice from 'doctors' that said it was too 'dangerous' to ride, he was a 'bloody awful patient, useless, screaming like a banshee cat'.

It wasn't the try-out he thought it would be, but Oliver got the job. He found Fred chilling – actually frightening – and inspiring in equal measure. Schooling horses, this fledgling amateur jockey with a handful of winners found himself upsides the inimitable John Francome and realised that 'throwing' horses at fences wouldn't do, they needed to learn how to do it themselves, in tight, at speed. This discovery came in the form of Fred yelling at him, 'DON'T DO THAT! HE'S A YOUNGSTER! HE'S GOT TO LEARN TO FIDDLE'. When Oliver was about to board Venture to Cognac in the 1979 Sun Alliance Novices' Hurdle for his first Festival ride, his dad said, 'Enjoy yourself Oliver.' Fred was immediately on hand to bark, 'Of course he can't enjoy it now! He can enjoy it afterwards. This is a serious business.'

Oliver also says you wouldn't find a kinder man than Fred, with a twinkle in his eye, a talent-spotter supreme – Richard Pitman,

John Francome, Charlie Brooks were just some of the names that passed through his hands – and a zero-tolerance policy for anyone playing what Oliver calls 'the giddy arse'. 'One day, I didn't turn up because I'd overslept, it was a snowy, frosty day so we didn't pull out on time, but he drove down and knocked on my door.' Long story short: it never happened again.

He worked for Fred for six years, married Fred's daughter then set up as a trainer in the same village and to this day, he keeps the same routine – easy days, work, schooling and road work – and he and Nicky have been true friends ever since. He regularly solicits Nicky's advice, admires him, and regularly reminds the six-time champion trainer that 'he's never won a National, and I don't mean the Grand National, I mean any National'.

* * *

The due diligence that Nicky applied when buying his first yard from his pal the trainer Roger Charlton, amounted to no more than Roger saying, 'Why don't you buy Windsor House?' and Nicky replying, 'That's a good idea.' The deal was done over steak and chips.

Happy Warrior would come with him. Next, he needed a head lad. Corky had been a mainstay at Fred's for years, overlapping with Nicky. He was working elsewhere when Nicky knocked on his door one evening. Corky squinted at him and after a while said, 'Henderson, isn't it? What can I do for you?' He'd never found out his first name.

'He sat down for a drink and said, "I'm going training,"' Corky remembers. '"Good for you, what's it got to do with me?"' It took a second attempt the following night, this time with a bottle of whisky, to persuade him. Word got out and Corky remembers how dismissive Fred's lads were about the news. 'We were a laughing stock. Corky as head lad and Nicky as trainer! What a joke.' And yet, Corky became Nicky's head lad, and the arrangement would stay in place for 41 years, sparking the most glittering career.

2

ZONGALERO

The gentle giant, so nearly a Grand National winner

UNLIKE THE wit and whimsy of most personal ads, Nicky's idea to place one in the racing pages of the Kerry local paper in 1979 had a no-time-to-explain, exciting scent of desperation: 'Tommy Carberry please ring Nicky Henderson.' Also, unlike most personal ads, it was 100 per cent successful.

Nicky was in a bind. A brand-new trainer, impatient to make his mark, with a feeling that the first horse entrusted to him could be destined for greatness. When Zongalero arrived to open Nicky's career at Windsor House, he already knew him as 'a very good horse in his younger days, and he'd been over fences and was doing quite well'. His owner, David Montagu, had one condition; jockey Steve Smith-Eccles must ride him in all his races. It was an unusual proviso, and Steve says now, 'I've never heard of that before, it was quite extraordinary and it got my foot in the door.'

Steve had ridden the horse at his previous yard and says, 'He was massive, about 17 hands and he looked spectacular.' He was also a 'big baby. I was cantering up the gallops one day and he got five to seven lengths behind and he started whinnying as the horses in front were leaving him behind. That gave me an idea of his character.' He didn't find it endearing, 'I knew if he put it in, he could win all these races,' he says. 'He won one big race, [the

Mandarin Handicap Chase at Newbury] but he always finished second, he didn't have the strength or the guts to see it through and when I think of the whinnying I can understand why. I'm the jockey, I'm on top and I know what he's capable of and what he could do if he put his best foot forward but he didn't, he bottled out every time.'

Corky bristles to hear a bad word about any of his horses, always defends them, and says, 'He wasn't soft, he was a lovely, old fashioned National Hunt type.' Nicky concedes Zongalero was 'a bit soft', but also 'special, kind and lovely. He was a magnificent horse.' His all-seeing eye saw something else in him and he suggested to David that this horse would love Aintree, and that they should go straight to the Grand National, rather than the Topham (one circuit not two). 'My suspicion was he wouldn't do it twice,' he remembers, 'and I was right, he hated it. He was that sort of horse, though I took him hunting to try and get him motivated. He was a two-and-a-half-mile horse, and in those day that's what you wanted for the National, a big strong horse that jumped and had the speed.' David agreed with the plan and Nicky set about working back from the Grand National to prep Zongalero.

A week before the race, Steve broke his neck racing at Exeter. A catastrophe for most, but almost more of an annoyance to this jockey. Likewise, when he fractured vertebrae in his back, it was a huge inconvenience ('it stopped me being champion jockey – and I was flying that year') and neither of those injuries was his worst. 'The most painful injury was when I had a fall and I was rolling along the ground and a horse behind me kicked me on my kneecap and split it,' he says.

So Zongalero was in the Grand National but Steve was reluctantly out, and the only other jockey that had been riding for Nicky was Bob Davies, but since he'd clinched the 1978 National on Lucius for Gordon Richards the previous year, he wasn't taking requests.

* * *

In 1975, carrying a lucky snail shell given to him by the owner's daughter, Tommy Carberry had partnered L' Escargot again in the most famous steeplechase in the world. The pair had been third in the National for the ages when Red Rum vanquished Crisp, and he wasn't planning on repeating that.

L' Escargot ran in blinkers which in those days could be the sign of a scoundrel, and he raced like he'd been shot out of a cannon. The two nearly parted company at the fence after Becher's, Tommy was briefly around the horse's neck like a wreath, but he recovered his poise and afterwards said the misstep had merely woken the horse up. They jumped the third last with Red Rum, whose jockey Brian Fletcher urged Tommy to crack on without him, he was all out. A classic ruse; sometimes (rarely) true and sometimes (usually) a bluff. Tommy knew Brian wanted a target for Red Rum to chase so he cooled his jets until the last, landing and thundering to a 15-length win. Denying the people's hero Red Rum his third title may have muted the welcome to the winner's enclosure, a reception with which Tommy was familiar, not to say immune. He had previously beaten Arkle, a horse so famous he received fan-mail to 'Himself, Ireland', in the Massey-Ferguson Gold Cup with Flying Wild in 1964. Tommy was a brilliant horseman, as well as brave, tactical and patient.

L' Escargot became the first Irish-trained winner of the Grand National since Mr What in 1958 and when he arrived home afterwards, he allegedly enjoyed the classic 'breakfast of champions' of a dozen eggs and champagne, Tommy's big night celebrating the win began at the Adelphi in Liverpool. It would be 24 years until the next Irish-trained Grand National winner and that was Bobbyjo, trained by Tommy and ridden by his son Paul, who literally swung from the rafters in the weighing room afterwards. Tommy became one of just four (including Fred Winter) who'd ridden and trained a Grand National winner and maybe the first to leap out of a car's open roof and onto the horse, still clutching a bottle of champagne, when parading Bobbyjo in County Meath. He was twice Irish champion jockey, five-time champion National Hunt jockey, and all of this while running a cattle farm near Dublin and being a father to six. In short: the big-race jockey.

* * *

'I rang up David and said "We've got a problem",' Nicky remembers, '"We've got no jockey." He said, "What are you going to do?" I said, "Well, I've been through the whole race, and the top 40 jockeys have all got a ride in the race. There's only one missing, and that's Carberry." "Why don't we get him?" "Well, I've tried to, he's in Ireland" – this was before mobile phones – "and I was told he was down in Kerry."' So Nicky placed his ad asking for a call and it came.

'He said, "Right, what can I do for you?" I said, "Looking through the runners, I don't think you've got a ride in the Grand National." He said, "I haven't." "Well, that's good news. How would you like to ride Zongalero?" "Not fussed." "Well, would you like to ride him?" He probably thought I had no idea what I was doing which was probably right. So, he said, "Not bothered."

'In those days it was an unwritten rule that the jockeys got another hundred quid on top for riding in the Grand National, just because it was special.' Nicky persisted, '"Well, wouldn't you like to ride him?" He said, "I'm too old for cheap thrills." Those were his words, I promise you! Too old for cheap thrills! I said, "Well, what's not cheap, then?" So, he quoted me a price, which was absolutely exorbitant. I said, "Tommy, you'll have to leave it with me." I told David that Tommy has agreed to ride him, but he wants – I'm not going to quote you the amount – it was three figures. So back to Tommy, I said, "OK, you're on. The only condition is I want you on the race course, 7.30 on Saturday morning." He'd never sat on Zongalero so, I said, "go and sit on him, have a canter round – you can't jump fences – at least you'll know what you're on. Mighty, big horse. You'll love him.'"

Nicky had saved the day, but that only made room for another group of 24 hours in need of rescue. The night before the race, Gordon Richards told Nicky that his big hope Lucius had a bruised foot and couldn't run – dreams dashed, just like that – so Bob Davies was free. Horses rarely pass up a chance to injure themselves. Bob had ridden Nicky's first ever winner, Dukery, in 1978 (beating Fred Winter's All Amber by 20 lengths in the Novices' Hurdle at Uttoxeter), he knew Zongalero as 'a lovely, big horse, a bit soft for fences', as he'd already schooled him. For jockeys, getting to know a horse takes exactly the amount of time that they have available. Sir AP McCoy OBE once picked up a spare ride at the Cheltenham Festival on Noble Prince and 'didn't even know what the horse looked like' when he walked into the parade ring. Bob says, 'You can get to know a horse in a couple of minutes of being on their back, how they move and gallop, once you've jumped a couple of fences. You can get used to a horse going to the start.' Bob also knew Nicky well. He remembers, 'In those days he was very nervy; the joke was he used to smoke a lot and there was never any ash on his cigarette in the paddock because it was shaken off.'

* * *

Bob was proper old school; maintaining an unnaturally low weight like a supermodel and hacking his way through problems that would floor most. First up: he had to stop drinking tea aged ten as it made him feel sick and tea plus double-digit sugars is a classic jockey meal. Second, he weighed ten stone aged 15. His natural weight was way over his riding weight and as a result he learned more about saunas and Turkish baths than any manager of a five-star spa. He had a sauna installed in every house he ever owned until he retired. He lived on boiled eggs and coffee (what he describes as high protein, low carb, 'the same basis as the Atkins diet'), and sipping Guinness to avoid cramps. He was always 5lbs dehydrated, driving between races with the heating on, in a sweatsuit. The regular dieter's goal of 1lb a week weight loss through a sensible meal plan is beyond a jockey's understanding. At home, he'd sweat off 4lbs in an hour with a hot bath, or five in two hours in the sauna (at 60° to 65°, 'not a high temp, I'd read a book'). It's hard to imagine Sebastian Coe, who that same year would set a world record over 1,500m at Zurich's Weltklasse meeting, following the same plan to stay lean.

* * *

Nicky's nightmare rolled on. 'I got hold of Bob, said, "Sorry about that, do you want to ride Zongalero?" He said, "Of course I do." "So, we've got a problem, I've got Carberry. You ride for me, I'll get hold of Carberry." Tommy wasn't getting an early night, and could have been in any bar in the whole of Aintree. Anywhere. I've got messages out everywhere – "Carberry ring Henderson". Again!'

He found Tommy, and come the morning, the two champion jockeys met Nicky on the race course at 7.30am, ready to canter one Zongalero. "'I'll tell you what we'll do,'" Nicky said, "'Bob, you'll ride him, but you're going to have to split the fee and any winnings with Tommy." "Absolutely fine." But what he didn't realise was how big the riding fee was. Half the riding fee that Tommy was getting was more than any other jockey was getting at the race, so Bob was delighted to get on, he was already miles ahead! And, I said to Tommy, "Here's half the riding fee, and you'll get half what Bob wins. Off back to bed, thank you very much!" Tommy was happy. He'd said he was too old for cheap thrills but he had a cheap thrill and all he had to do was get up in the morning, turn up at the race course, collect a lot of money and go back to bed!'

* * *

All of this, to get one horse, with one jockey, to the start of one race, on one day for one owner. Nicky had five horses in training in the early days, and now trains around 150, and every single one requires this much effort every day in one way or another. It might have been the first time, but it was by no stretch of the imagination the last time that he would go to great lengths.

Over the decades he would, for example, sell a horse to a man in surprising surroundings. 'We were doing the unveiling of the Grand National weights, and there was a wonderful character called Ivan Straker who was the boss of Seagram,' Nicky remembers. 'I knew Ivan pretty well by then, and I said, "Ivan I need a word with you." We were actually in the gents' loo. Ivan had a great booming voice: "Suppose you want to sell me a horse!" "Well, yes, actually I do – I've got just the horse for you." I told him all about it, he bought The Tsarevich for £18,000.' The horse won at the Cheltenham Festival two years on the trot, and finished second in the 1987 Grand National, when Seagram was sponsoring it.

In 1981, he would train Sun Lion to win the Hunters' Chase at Warwick for Robert Waley-Cohen, a very dear friend, one of his owners and then still an amateur jockey. 'I'll never forget it,' he says. 'Robert's the first to admit, he was a very good rider – hunting and that sort of thing – but he wasn't a jockey. I've known Robert for millions of years. We managed to train a horse for him to ride a winner on, which I consider one of my greatest feats.'

He'd also go on to take delight in his 50-1 winner On the Blind Side in a three-mile handicap hurdle at Newbury in 2023. The horse had long lost his way, and Nicky found a route back, by sending him out hacking instead of training to 'get him to believe that life is still fun'.

And he would refuse to give up when his star Spirit Son collapsed in a paddock, couldn't get up, and vets couldn't see any future for the horse. While the horse's groom Hannah kept vigil, they built an outdoor stable for him where he lay, with hay bales and a canopy borrowed from a friend's marquee hire company, then called on vet Celia Marr, who arrived after nightfall. She sent Nicky home and said if she couldn't get the horse on his feet by morning, she would reluctantly have to agree with the original vets. At 3am Nicky received a two-word text: 'He's up.'

* * *

Back at Aintree, the final piece of the jigsaw, the actual race. Bob remembers how magnificently Zongalero rose to the occasion. Some horses just take to it. 'He was fantastic,' he says. 'There's a picture of him jumping Becher's and there's about six inches of daylight between his belly and the top of the fence. He never even nodded his head when he landed.'

The fences were famously bigger in those days, and the horses jumped them differently. Bob says, 'Horses used to go in and steady up to jump fences about two foot thick; you couldn't stand off and jump, they tended to shorten a stride, rather than as normally lengthening their stride. Red Rum shortened his stride before a fence, to use his hocks to jump.'

Someone who was in the crowd that day remembers, 'As they jumped the last, three horses were absolutely together, Rubstic on the stand side, Zongalero in the middle and Rough and Tumble on the inside. Rough and Tumble had been making the strongest challenge and at that point I thought he would win, but at the Elbow it was obvious that he was very tired and he dropped back. That left Rubstic and Zongalero. Of the two, the latter had up till now looked the stronger, but on that long run-in it was Rubstic who finally got ahead and held on to win. A tremendously exciting climax to a very dramatic race. Yet Rubstic was not a particularly popular winner. More people seemed to be cheering for Zongalero than for him, and his reception in the unsaddling enclosure was tepid compared to some I have witnessed.'

Zongalero had taken the opportunity to bruise his foot a few weeks before and his training hadn't been usual. The blacksmith gave the horse a wider shoe to protect more of his hoof, and after Nicky cantered him in the mornings, Corky swam him in the afternoons to keep him off the ground. Bob says, 'He was fantastic all through the race, he got leg-weary after the second-last. If he'd been ridden the week before, he'd have won, I could feel him getting tired, at the last furlong. His legs didn't set in until we crossed the Melling Road – crossing it, I thought he'd win, then before the last all of sudden that was it.'

He always saw his role as a jockey to 'encourage them as much as possible. It's back to horsemanship, ride the race however the horse is going, not how you want to ride it. If it doesn't suit your horse how it's going, if it's too fast, even if you're told to make the running, it's no good chasing them, you go at the speed your horse is comfortable with and hope it works out.' John Francome has the same view and regularly advises young jockeys that they should spend two of every three minutes thinking about what the horse is doing, 'Because he's doing all the work, how much petrol is he using, even going to the start? You should be getting there at a time your horse can get there, your job is to make sure you don't get to the end of a race and your horse can't put one leg in front of the other; most of the time you should know.'

* * *

Zongalero was pipped into second by just over a length. The winning time was nine minutes, 52.9 seconds, a way off from both the fastest time set by Mr Frisk in 1990 with eight minutes 47.8 seconds, and the slowest (Lottery in the inaugural year of 1839 in 14 minutes 53 seconds, though that race included a stone wall, ploughed field and a finish over two hurdles). Over the decades, the drop on the landing side of Becher's has been repeatedly adjusted, finally reduced from three feet to ten inches, the distance to the first fence has been reduced to slow the cavalry charge, and the unforgiving timber frame of the top of the fences has been replaced with 15 inches of plastic birch. These amendments have all made a positive difference, not to the average number of finishers, but the number of fallers and the number of deaths. When the fences changed in 2013, Pineau de Re won in nine minutes 9.9 seconds, Tiger Roll's second win in 2019 was the same time as Red Rum's first win, and only Many Clouds has come close to the record when he won the 2015 race in eight minutes 56.9 seconds. So there hasn't been a steady increase in speed, and research has shown that the last great leap forward when race times significantly improved was at the turn of the century, when jockeys changed their riding style to sit up off the horse's back, isolating themselves from the horse's movement. It made racing much harder work for the jockeys, it took less out of the horses, and race times improved by up to seven per cent.

Associate Professor Dr Jane Williams, head of research at Hartpury University in Gloucestershire says, 'Shortening the stirrups, and increasing the weight above and over the horse's back allows you to use the back. If you think about the horse, it's a rear-wheel drive car, if you like. So, you've got the big backside at the end, all the muscles on the backside, and the legs are what's generating all the power. Then the pelvis is almost a conduit, and the spine needs to be flexible to be able to give a bit of lateral bending, side-to-side, but also needs to be strong enough to be able to channel that energy through to the front. And then the front leg has the elastic capacity to be able to drive it. So being able to free up the spine, and allow the horse to use itself effectively by taking the rider's weight off it, really improves the speed. Racing predominantly is about galloping and jumping, so to be able to gallop well, you need to be able to transfer the energy through, but also to bio-mechanically allow the horse to operate to its full potential. Taking the rider slightly out of it does that.'

That accounts for the better race times, and the lack of any major gains since then may be because, as Kate Allen, Royal College of Veterinary Surgeons recognised specialist in equine sports medicine at Bristol University says, 'We have probably reached peak speed. There are still massive advances in human athletes and it's interesting we're not reaching that with horses, despite horses being genetically targeted and bred for that single purpose, whereas humans are mostly by chance – if you happen to have genetically gifted parents. It's weird in a breed that is bred to get faster that it's not getting faster. Partly, we're close to their physiological limit, and despite advances in heart rate monitoring, training hasn't really changed, and we're pretty close to what a horse can sustain and endure.'

* * *

Zongalero ended the year with a second in the Hennessy Gold Cup at Newbury with Steve Smith-Eccles, and a win with Bob Davies in the Mandarin Handicap Chase, also at Newbury in December. The next year, the gentle giant went back to the Grand National and 'did what I feared he might do,' Nicky says. 'That's why I did it the first year. He was a bit soft, I used to ride him every day at home. I adored him. Mind, we only had five horses so it wouldn't have been difficult to pick one.'

Charlie Mann started working for Nicky in 1979 and stayed for six years as a conditional jockey and continued riding out for him after that. He rode Zongalero at home and remembers, 'He looked a dream of a horse, big strong physique, but he didn't have it upstairs. He was a big soft git and when he went back to Aintree for the second time, he didn't want to get off the horse-box when he saw where he was!'

Gemma Pearson is a veterinary equine behaviourist in charge of the equine behaviour service at the Royal (Dick) School of Veterinary Studies, Edinburgh and says, 'This is a context-specific response. Arriving at Aintree will have triggered a certain emotional response, obviously a negative emotional one! It does not mean that he made a conscious decision or "knew" where he was. But that the specific environment triggered his emotional response subconsciously.'

Research has shown that a horse's associative memory is almost photographic, so they can link something good (or bad) to a place, and they even have 'single trial aversion learning' which means that once something bad has happened, they log it and see no need to revisit or reclassify the risk.

Finally coaxed from the lorry, on his second attempt at the Grand National fences Zongalero didn't enjoy it at all and refused at fence 20. The third time he came into the race, having been pulled up in the Hennessy Gold Cup and the Welsh National, he fell at fence 22. Steve Smith-Eccles rode him in both of these returns and remembers, 'He must have been a very intelligent horse. He knew where he was. He jumped the first circuit as though he owned the place and as soon as he went to the second circuit he thought, oh I don't like this, no thank you. You could feel him falling away, and there was nothing I could do about it. Every fence he came to he kept putting on the brakes, putting on the brakes. The nature of Becher's is if you didn't get far enough on the landing side out of it, you were in trouble and he fell.'

Steve concludes, 'He was a great horse but he didn't have the guts of a class horse. Nick trained him to the best of his ability but mentally he didn't have the guts to bring out that last bit of ability. He'd have been a superstar.'

* * *

This was the start of Nicky's career, when he'd still call on Fred for his sage advice. 'He said, if things are going wrong, don't change them because you've proved it works. If they aren't running right, which they often don't, and in those early years when that happened, you panic, what am I doing wrong? He'd say sweat it out. And most of it is instinct, you have a rough idea of what you're trying to do every morning before you start.'

It was also the beginning of long, collaborative partnerships with his stable jockeys. Even 40-odd years later, he has only had a handful; Steve, Mick Fitzgerald, Barry Geraghty and now Nico de Boinville. It's unusual, and a very positive thing, that they've all stayed for so many years. He says, 'I've been very lucky, in that I haven't had many, I've had a lot of very happy marriages that have gone on for a long time and a lot of good jockeys have been through our hands. Nico arrived at the same time as David Bass, Andrew Tinkler and Jerry McGrath, and they all went on to make it. Fantastic! Good for them. It made them competitive, if they wanted the rides, they had to be good, they had to work very hard to be the blue-eyed boy.'

Steve was his first stable jockey, and there was nothing in Steve's childhood to suggest he'd be a rider, let alone a champion. He was born and bred in Pinxton, a mining village in Derbyshire but as a very young boy, horses sent their signal. 'I walked by my father and uncle watching racing on a black and white TV one Saturday afternoon and I said, "Dad, I'm going to be a jockey when I grow up," and I carried on walking. That's where the seed was planted. I had no connection with horses whatsoever.'

He was 14, and not the first to look blankly at the school careers' advisor, so his mother wrote to three trainers ('I don't know where she got the names from'). Arthur Stephenson wasn't looking for apprentices, Frenchie Nicholson wouldn't take a pound over 6st 7lbs, and Steve had been delivering hundredweight bags of coal for a friend's dad so he was a monstrous 7st 10lbs, and Harry Thomson Jones offered a month's trial. Steve has kept the letter; racing has romance in its bones.

Week one he fed the pigs on the muck heap, polished the brass on head-collar buckles and swept the yard, and week two he trotted round a sand ring on a horse, 'bouncing up and down, my arse was so sore'. Week three, he was following everyone else in the string up the gallops. 'All of a sudden, the penny dropped and I thought aye-aye, I know how to do this,' he remembers. 'Within three months of not seeing a racehorse I rode a gallop with a guy called Lester Piggott. I was on the lead horse, I made the running and he came by me as though I was standing still. Everything then became easy, I don't want to be blasé, that's the way it was.'

* * *

Nicky had 22 winners in his first year and he says, 'To be second in the Grand National in your first year, I suppose, was a huge boost. It was a whirlwind, we had a very good year, we started with five horses and grew and grew. It certainly helped, in that it gave you the profile that owners probably liked.'

What stayed with Nicky was the other side of the coin; not the thrill of coming second but the disappointment. He remembers the Sunday morning after the National, back at Windsor House, and trainer Barry Hills drove in. 'We thought we'd come and say hello,' he announced. Barry Hills had been to the airport to collect a tiny little American teen called The Kid, aka Stevie Wonder, aka the Six Million Dollar man, aka Steve Cauthen. He was young (18), tiny (5ft 1in, though he grew) and famous. He'd ridden his first racing gallop as a five-year-old, his first race in 1976 and in 1977 he'd clocked up 487 winners, and was the first jockey to win $6 million in one year. In 1978 he was the youngest rider to win the Triple Crown on Affirmed and then he hit a slump, and struggled with weight, so he decided to move to England (the weights are a little higher) and was brought over by Robert Sangster to ride. He became a great friend of Nicky's, was champion jockey three times, won the 2000 Guineas, the Epsom Derby twice, St Leger three times, among many other shimmering prizes. 'Let's go and have a look at Zongalero,' they said. Steve had only ever ridden nifty flat horses and had never seen one this size, and asked, wide-eyed, 'Is that a … racehorse?'

Barry's impromptu visit was a kind one. He was familiar with how it felt nearly winning a prestigious, high-profile race, having come close in the Epsom Derby enough times to remember the sting. 'He knows what it's like; the winner is all over the front page, you're nowhere, you've put up a heroic performance but you're nobody.

'We were home alone,' Nicky says, 'the rest of the world was celebrating with the winner and we were sat there, dumbfounded. The excitement of the whole thing and we were nobody. We were nothing. You come so close.'

3

SEE YOU THEN

The foot-perfect triple Champion hurdle winner, savage in his stable

SEE YOU THEN's mix of personalities were so distinct and unrelated, they'd confuse the most experienced psychological profiler. One of them derailed his destiny. His breeding was meant to lead him straight into the stalls for the Derby. His sire was the courageous Royal Palace, who won the 2000 Guineas and the Epsom Derby in 1967 among others, and then the King George VI & Queen Elizabeth Stakes, his last race, where he broke down inside the final furlong, but stayed the course, finishing lame. See You's career on the flat never materialised because he was so savage, even as a yearling, that he was gelded, 'which is a good thing. Colts can get nasty, geldings very seldom do,' Nicky says, but it didn't cure his ferocious temper, which he carried with him his entire life. He won half of his eight starts on the flat and both of his hurdle races in Ireland for trainer Con Collins before arriving at Nicky's yard as a four-year-old hurdler, bought by Nicky's vet, the late Frank Mahon, and en route to Italy where his owners lived.

It was just a few weeks before the 1984 Cheltenham Festival and he wasted no time showcasing his personality. He had strong views about people barging into his stable. 'You'd go into his box,' Nicky remembers, 'he'd grab you and while you were turning to get out of his way, he'd kick you! Both ends!'

He was, to put it mildly, grumpy. 'We put boots on him one morning and it took a day to get them off!' Nicky says. 'From then on, the most wonderful Glyn Foster who had been in racing for centuries looked after him. He was the only one who could go into the box. It was his kingdom; out of it he was putty in your hands.' Glyn found a way with him. Steve Smith-Eccles became his jockey and says he deserved the Victoria Cross for putting up with him. He says, 'I wouldn't go in his box; the first time I did with Nicky, he tore the shirt off his back.'

He must have had his reasons. Corky says, 'He was probably treated badly when he was a yearling, he must have been, horses aren't naturally like that. The only way I could get bandages onto him was if he was loose in the stable; if I tied him up, he'd pin me against the wall and kick or bite. Or both.' Outside his stable? 'An absolute gent.'

See You Then was just passing through, and Nicky already had the apple of his eye, 'the best four-year-old in England at the time, Chilldown, who I absolutely adored'. Come the day of the Triumph Hurdle, both horses lined up. John Francome was aboard Chilldown, and as they passed the stands for the first time, the horse broke down. Peter O'Sullevan interrupted his rhythmic commentary by saying with shock, 'something's happened to Chilldown, I'm very much afraid he's broken a leg and been pulled up by John Francome'. There were no green screens in those days, so Northern Game and See You Then would gallop past a bright green tarpaulin being held up to shield the stricken horse on the second loop.

'Chilldown broke his leg in front of us,' Nicky recalls. 'I went straight down to him, and it was blatantly obvious he was going to have to be put down. I was there holding him and they came round the next time, See You Then was in second place over the last hurdle and went off up the hill. I could hear the noise, I thought he'd won and I couldn't give a hoot. Chilldown was here and he was dead.' John stayed with the horse until the end too, and remembers standing right by him and as the vet pulled the trigger, 'the horse put his head down and the bullet went off into the stands, it was a wonder it didn't kill somebody'.

It was a photo finish, and See You Then was pipped into second, but Nicky didn't mind, 'It didn't matter one jot. It was brutal.' He was distraught, tears streaming down his face. 'I adored Chilldown,' Nicky says. Because he was a star? No, 'Because he was the most charming character you'd ever come across, gorgeous, such a kind horse.' Before anything else, it's an emotional relationship between Nicky and his horses.

National Hunt trainer Richard Phillips was just starting out in his career when he saw the disaster play out. 'It was the first time I saw the Nicky Henderson emotions,' he remembers, 'he had See You Then, second in the Triumph Hurdle, but he was down at the last, walking away from Chilldown who had died. The vision of a successful young trainer bursting into uncontrollable tears at the loss of a horse struck me, he was absolutely in bits, and it took me aback.' That's how it is for Nicky, 'I'm terrible, I'm the worst,' he says, 'on a racecourse, the very great days get to you the same as the dreaded days when you lose a friend. That's my make-up and I can't change it.'

Decades on from that day at Cheltenham, Richard says now, 'That's probably one of the reasons why Nicky's good at what he does, he gets quite attached to them.' It's understandable, too, 'The fact horses are so good to you makes it terribly emotional,' he says. Richard has his own way of dealing with it. 'With anything serious I'm very cool. When someone's left the wrong coloured blanket out I go mental; it doesn't matter to anyone but me, but with a death I become very professional. It's my job to make it the best situation it can possibly be.' When he lost a horse at Newbury at the third last, he walked away alone. 'I had my tears between the two- and one-furlong markers, by the time I reached the grandstand, I was alright. It's the horse, it's the people, it's what you've created, the places the horse has taken you, you feel responsible.'

And anyway, 'I think all the best trainers are emotional people, wearing their hearts on their sleeves,' he says, 'being emotional means understanding how the horses think.' As an example, he remembers giving an after-dinner speech for the late Sir Henry Cecil's staff, and during the evening, he told Henry about his horse, Time Won't Wait. He'd been brought down at that year's Cheltenham Festival right in front of him. He thought he'd broken his jaw, which was fixable, but he wasn't getting better and he was worried, and due to collect a new drip from the Royal Veterinary College on the way home. The next morning, Richard had breakfast with Henry and was 'asking all the questions a young trainer would and I was just thinking, I need to leave to get the drip, and Henry stopped mid-sentence and said, "You want to go, you're worried about your horse."'

* * *

See You wasn't alone in having a flash of temper. John Francome, the man who can say with no false modesty, 'I back my judgement with horses every time. I can get a tune out of any horse, any saddle, any bridle, any time. With anything else, I have no idea, but I've spent my life with horses and I know them,' had a horse with a fury.

'I bought Poet to go jumping,' he remembers, 'I was grooming him one day, doing everything right, he had a rug on keeping him warm, and he turned around and picked me up by my chest and he was bloody strong. He got hold of skin.

'That was just him, I never felt like giving up on him. He'd have frightened most people,' but not John because, 'the second they know you're scared of them, you've had it.' Poet's rage was quick, conversation-ending, indiscriminate. 'Some lad was showing off one night, he said to Poet, "you don't frighten me" and the horse bit his finger off.'

Only a couple of people could even get a bridle on him and plenty of times, when they planned to ride out, they couldn't even do that. 'He taught me that if you get one big and strong enough and he doesn't want to do something, he won't do it.'

Still, this is *the* John Francome, so it's no surprise, that, 'we got a tune out of him in the end. You find a way round most of the time. You'll never win falling out with them every day. Like people, it's about finding a way without force to get them to do what you want, that fits in with them.' He describes him as nothing more than 'misguided' and says, 'I don't know what his background was; something had gone wrong in his life somewhere but when he was here you could never trust him.' That said, 'I loved him. He had a proper character, and he was a brilliant jumper. Other horses have come and gone, but he's still remembered in the yard. I miss him.'

* * *

See You's shenanigans continued. Did it ever occur to Nicky to give up on him? 'Not at all, we had a job to do.' Somehow, while making no demands at all, horses also insist that their high-maintenance lifestyle is never compromised (they'll know if you cut corners and are usually satisfied with the best of everything) and their many complex, often eccentric needs, are all met. Stoic Glyn tied a stable rubber (looks like a tea towel, used to polish a horse's coat) to the top of his head-collar to distract him. Nicky's knitwear was fish-netted courtesy of the horse's piano-key teeth and 'the back end worked as well, both hind legs. He got me every which way. I treated him with huge respect but I couldn't go into the box on my own with him. He hated me! I loved him and he hated me. It didn't matter, I could live with it, as long as Glyn was there.'

His natural talent sweetened the pill. Nicky describes his 'unique ability to cross hurdles at speed like an arrow' and is still awestruck even now. 'It was like watching those Olympic athletes jumping a hurdle – they're so deadly accurate with the ability to do it so quickly – gone – and it's not the jumping, it's the crossing at speed.' He only schooled him once a year, and only over four hurdles. Partly because he didn't need the practice, and partly because he had legs as sturdy as twigs. Charlie Mann rode him at home and describes him as a nutcase. 'He pulled quite hard, he was horrible, tried to savage you, a mental case, I didn't want to give him his feed at night. It didn't stop him being an amazing athlete, an extraordinarily talented horse with legs like glass.'

* * *

Schooling mornings were, according to John Francome, tense, and still are now, as Nicky's horses thunder into view, onlookers like Mick Fitzgerald, AP McCoy, Corky, all seeing what mortals miss, and Nicky muttering 'far too fast … far too fast' as they stream over the fences, before breakfast (black coffee taken standing up for the jockeys), as the day's plans are made. John says, 'He's worried something's going to go wrong, horses all over the place like Fred Karno's army. If he stayed in and had a cup of coffee things would go better. He's a born worrier.' The schooling's so crucial because, as Charlie says, 'If they don't jump, they don't win races. They have to enjoy it and when you school them you lay them open to being injured, so if the horse does it well, you stop schooling.'

The tension was contagious; James Nixon worked as a stable lad for Nicky and remembers his first, nervous, attempt. He'd come from showjumping so he had 'a rough idea but it's a bit different going 30mph not 10mph'. A few years ago, he had dislocated his shoulder when Nico de Boinville called. 'Where are you?' Nico asked. 'Oaksey House,' (where injured jockeys go to be repaired) James replied. 'Perfect, can you ride out this week?' 'No problem.' An exchange only two jockeys could have, his dislocated shoulder not even mentioned. James thought, you don't get to ride at Nicky Henderson's very often. His horse had never seen a hurdle before and decided to jump the wing instead.

* * *

See You travelled to Italy, as was always planned, won his Gran Series de Quattro Anno Champion Hurdle and returned to Windsor House for the winter – no softer for his taste of *la dolce vita* – as he needed the ministrations of vet Frank Mahon. He'd been beaten just before Cheltenham and he wasn't the red-hot favourite come the 1985 Champion Hurdle. John Francome was due to ride, having taken over the season before when Nicky and stable jockey Steve Smith-Eccles had 'the first of our divorces'. Nicky says, 'We had about three. He lived in Newmarket, it was too difficult and he was doing his own thing, and I wasn't in control of the situation, he was, and I'm not a control freak, but that's the wrong way round. I love Steve, he's a great mate. He was a wild child, not a run of the mill stable jockey.' He remembers schooling one day, when he 'gave Steve a bollocking: "Wake up! Get hold of your horse! Make him jump!" and he got off and said "ride it yourself" and chucked the reins at me!' At this point, at Cheltenham, they were non-speakers.

Steve says of those days as a young jockey, 'It's hard to explain, I was a Jack the lad, I could take anything anyone could throw at me.

Every time I went to work, I knew there was a possibility I wouldn't be coming home in one piece. That happened quite a few times, I lived every day as my last, I worked hard and played hard and I loved it.' He found Nicky 'more apprehensive, more sensible. He ran a professional training yard, that's what's made him so successful now, that's the way he started. It was a strange relationship, we got on well, and at the end of the day I rode him masses of winners.'

Come the race day, everything was in place. John was riding The Reject for Fred Winter in the Arkle the race before, and the horse took a tumble. As he rose, John got his foot caught in his stirrup leather and was 'hung up', suspended upside down, with his head hanging inches from the horse's steel-shod feet.

John remembers, 'It was a fall you couldn't have done in 100 tries; the horse fell and slid along the ground and as he rolled over my left leg went to the other side and the stirrup leather wrapped round my leg and he got up and my leg was hanging. My foot was through the stirrup iron, my leg wrapped round the leather. Luckily, I caught the reins before they went.'

Steve remembers the accident and says, 'If that horse had galloped off he would have been dead, fortunately one of the fence attendants ran over and caught the horse before he galloped on. If he'd gone, his head would have been banging against his back legs. It shocked John, he wasn't physically injured and there was nothing stopping him riding but he'd had enough. It must have scared him and he called it a day.' John was shaken up, and his choice not to ride the next race might be a museum-exhibit-rare example of a jockey making a decision to put their health and welfare first.

Steve says to get 'hung up' like that was highly unusual, but then, 'The Reject runs three weeks later at Chepstow, falls, John gets hung up again, once again the fence attendant saves him. He came back to the weighing room, threw his saddle on the bench and said, "Boys, that's me done, I'm off." He was mentally disturbed by it.' John had already decided that season would be his last, but after being hung up for a second time, he retired on the spot.

Back at Cheltenham, desperate times called for desperate measures. Nicky was an old hand at not taking no for an answer. He was at the Festival, with See You Then, but without a jockey. 'I thought, now what am I going to do, no one else has sat on this horse. I went into the weighing room to see which jockey hadn't got a ride in the Champion Hurdle and there was only one man sat there – Ec.' Nicky calls nearly everyone he knows by a nickname (John Francome is Frank), and Steve Smith-Eccles is Ec.

'So I said, "Steve, come on, you're going to ride See You Then." He said, "Oh great guv." He didn't sound over-excited,' but he didn't know then what he would know a few minutes later.

Steve had never sat on this horse, but as a freelancer, he was used to it. 'When you jump on a horse and you pick up the reins, it's like a telegraph wire, from me to him and vice versa. If you've ridden thousands, as I did, that's the way it happens, I knew his form, he was just another horse, I knew how he liked to be ridden, and I went out and went through my paces.'

Nicky told him how to ride the race; John always rode whichever way he wanted, but as Steve had never sat on him, Nicky was concerned he'd hold him up too much. He needn't have worried. He gave the horse a 'beautiful ride'. The favourite Browne's Gazette jinked as the tapes went up, veering left then right, and took himself out of contention, denying his trainer Monica Dickinson the chance to become the first female champion trainer (the family had other glories, her son Michael had trained 12 winners on Boxing Day in 1982, and also, staggeringly, the first five home in the 1983 Gold Cup). And anyway, Steve says it wouldn't have made any difference, See You would have beaten anyone that day, he never put a foot wrong. He remembers, 'coming down to the last, I saw the one in front of me pushing and kicking away, I looked behind me, there's nothing that's going to beat me, I felt confident. I sat, sat, popped the last hurdle and half way up the run-in I gave him a little nudge, I don't think I even hit him with a stick, and that was it. It was so easy.'

The horse with the hell-cat temper had set himself right at every hurdle, had never mis-stepped, faltered or waned. He was perfect. Streaming past the post, seven lengths clear, he was the first of Nicky's Champion Hurdle winners (he has now won it more times than any other trainer), his first Festival winner, and helped him become champion trainer for the first time in 1985/86.

Corky remembers See You coming home after that mighty win, and vets congregating at the yard. 'His legs were swollen, they weren't pretty, and the vets were considering firing him.' Firing is a barbaric-sounding, now extinct process where hot irons are used on the area and as the skin heals and strengthens, it holds the tendons in place, and it requires a year off, but Corky wasn't having it and they agreed to give Corky time. 'He was mine for six weeks,' he remembers. Every day, he'd take See You to stand in the swimming pool, morning, noon and evening in freezing water for an hour at a time, sometimes he had to break the ice. When the vets returned, there was, miraculously, nothing to see.

Come the second year, See You was now a permanent resident, and his legs still weren't strong enough for more than one run max before defending his Champion Hurdle title. The scant appearances in public made him elusive. He ran five times in the previous season, three times in 1985/86 and twice in 1986/87, once in 1987/88, after which he retired, but that ended when he appeared again in 1989/90 (when he ran four times before a final retirement), the press took to calling him See You When, and he never quite won the hearts of race-goers, who choose their favourites with the certainty of teen girls crowning pop stars.

* * *

Steve was back riding for Nicky and remembers, 'Corky ran the roost, you had to get on with him or you wouldn't be in a job. We spoke the same language, he didn't take any prisoners and neither did I, we got on well.' Corky knew the horses so well, he only had to put his head over the stable door to know if there was a problem (he says a conservative ratio would be out of 60 horses, 15 might need attention, every day). He could tell which horses had exercised on all-weather tracks and which on the wood chip and no horse ever galloped without their legs being passed fit for service. Most of what Corky knew and knows, couldn't be taught. When another trainer's assistant asked him to look over one of his horses, Corky opened the stable door and said, 'I don't need to go any further.' 'But you haven't felt it.' 'I don't need to, a blind man could see,' and ran his hand down the horse's good leg. 'Not that one!' 'Is that so?' He ran his hand down the other and said, 'Forget the season.' Apart from finding the source of warmth, Corky, says the trick (learned from Frank Mahon), was simply not to press down hard on a horse's leg, but run a hand down slowly, gently, 'the same pressure all the way down, don't squeeze, down, down, down, then the other leg'.

He was uncompromising and says, 'The odd time Nicky stepped out of line, I showed my Irish side.' It wasn't just Nicky; when two lads arrived late to ride out one morning, Corky took them into the tack room individually, and gave them a verbal warning so strong it could have smelted the stirrup irons. It worked, but only for two days. On day three, they were still asleep in bed when they should have been riding. 'I filled two buckets of water,' Corky remembers, 'and one at a time, went into their rooms and said, "get up", and threw the bucket of water over them.' Unmoved by their hysterical screaming, he said, '"Get up and pack your bags and move out, or ride out." They couldn't go back to bed so they saddled up and ended up staying six years.'

Much later, Corky met them at Newbury. 'Thanks very much,' they said to him, 'We'd have been in jail, only for you, you put us on the right road,' and they all shook hands. His wife Diane remembers lads would say, 'If we were in trouble, it's because we were in trouble, not because he didn't like us.'

There's one way of doing things for Corky, and it's no surprise that it's the right way ('it takes the same time to do it wrong as right'). He's a legend in Lambourn, anyone would be honoured to have a horse in his unfailing care, which could be wrenchingly tender. The mighty Spartan Missile came to stay at Windsor House; the horse belonged to Nicky's then father-in-law John Thorne (Nicky and Diana were married for 28 years, had three daughters, Camilla, Tessa and Sarah and divorced in 2006). Spartan Missile developed such a serious leg problem that he had to be put down. He was due to be buried on the grounds. Corky remembers seeing his head over the stable door on the morning, ears pricked, looking around and thought with despair, oh, mate. He called the vet, led the horse to the huge grave that had been dug, and when the horse was laid to rest, one of his front legs was sticking straight out in front of him. 'Look, look,' Corky said, really distressed. Someone tried to reassure him that it was OK, now. 'No, it's not,' Corky said, and climbed down into the grave, tucked Spartan Missile's leg up under him, to make him comfortable, and straightened one of his ears that had been folded under his beautiful head.

* * *

Getting a fit and sound See You to a second Champion Hurdle the following year was a magnificent feat of training, and Corky's masterpiece. Steve remembers the ride and the horse's style, 'Three or four strides out, he'd jiggle his feet, he made it spot on every time, he never made a mistake, which is an amazing thing to say, I can't explain it. It makes it easy for the jockey, you can go anywhere with him. He always had to come from behind, he liked a lead to the last hurdle.' It's as vivid now as then. 'I didn't take up the running till half way up the run-in, I didn't hit the front till then, I knew that's the way he liked to do it, I was riding my race, looking around, seeing that one getting a slap down the shoulder, pushing along, the one in front I've got him beat, not to be blasé but it made it so easy for me to ride the race I knew he wanted.'

Charlie Mann says Nicky's skill with See You was that, 'he didn't take risks, and not many trainers would have kept him sound. He was very good with him, he was not an easy horse to train, because you've got to be so careful; every time you do fast work, you're open to injuring him, he had very fragile legs and one of Nicky's best training feats ever was getting See You Then on a course three years running. He was the master of it and still is.' Nicky says, 'There's a fascination to find something and to make it into something. I like to see the fruits of something done well.'

For See You's third Champion Hurdle, he made an appearance at Haydock, as preparation, in a race almost run for him, and he duly won and was back on as favourite for the Festival. But rather than being the confidence-boost that it sounds, it added more angst to Nicky's bill. As John Francome says, 'Horses have only got to be three per cent off their best to get beaten 20 lengths. If you ran the 800m with a cold you'd get lapped.'

So, at 6.30am, after a sleepless night worrying what state See You's tendons would be in, Nicky made for his stable. It was a

Sunday morning, the boys would be in at 8am, but Glyn would be in because he was always in and See You would be tired after his race and the journey home. Nicky had high hopes he might be able to get a head-collar on and even feel his tendons.

The stable door was wide open, Nicky assumed Glyn had already arrived, but it was Frank, the vet with the expert touch, sitting in the manger, pinned there by See You.

'Get me out of here, he's got me,' said this most experienced and eminent vet.

'I can't,' replied the Champion Hurdle-winning trainer, 'The back end kicks, the front end bites, we'll have to wait for Glyn.' See You's leg bandages were half off; he was disgusted to have been disturbed.

'At least he ate up,' said Frank gamely, squatting on the empty manger. Glyn arrived, like a Norland nanny scooping up the screaming baby from the frazzled parents, and trotted him up, safe and sound.

The yard had bent over backwards for this horse. Along with hours in the Windsor House pool, he'd worked all over the country. 'One day, the press was trying to find out where I was going,' Nicky remembers. 'They were waiting outside to follow the horse-box. So, I got a horse-box to leave 20 minutes earlier – empty – and they followed it. And then another one set off in the opposite direction with See You Then, to Weston-super-Mare to gallop on the beach. I didn't want them to see that we were in serious trouble.'

* * *

In the days before See You's 1987, third consecutive attempt (Steve is quite sure that 'if ever a horse was going to win a fourth Champion Hurdle it would have been him, if he hadn't damaged his hind leg just before at Wincanton'), Nicky's all-weather track was frozen.

Steve remembers his 'dedication … getting up and riding around on a tractor with a harrow at 3am to make sure that See You Then could canter round it at 8am. When you work with a guy like that you want to give them your best. I was a little bit wild in my day, but if I wasn't like that I wouldn't have been as successful as I was, it was the only way it could work for me.'

Come the race, Steve thought the horse might only have been at 95 per cent. 'I ran out of petrol 100 yards from the line. That was the one time he could have got beaten,' he says. 'He wasn't fully wound-up, because of the weather. The Flatterer should have beaten me, but his jockey left his challenge too late.' And See You Then was, again, faultless, 'He never put a foot wrong, he'd jink his legs, prick his ears and make sure he met every hurdle spot on. I get the accolades but my grandmother could have ridden him. To ride three consecutive Champion Hurdles on the same horse is quite extraordinary. I didn't think at the time how lucky I was. If The Reject hadn't fallen, John Francome would have ridden and I wouldn't be the person that I am.' Did the horse put Steve on the map? Not quite, 'I already had a huge career and I was rising through the ranks. I hit the big time around 1980, I knew where I was going.'

Such solid self-belief meant he also knew when to stop. 'If you make 40, as I did, that's a good innings. You know when you ride every 12 to 15 rides will be a fall and if you're 40 you're not going to take the injuries you have in the past. It was extraordinary; one morning I woke up and drove to Windsor to ride the red-hot favourite for James Fanshawe and I finished fourth. I came in and flung my saddle on the bench and said, "that's me done boys", and I never looked back. I didn't go out on a winner, but driving down I thought, I don't like this, I got beat and that was the final nail. I stopped when I wanted to.'

Sports psychologist Michael Caulfield says jockeys 'empty the tank over and over again to the point that they have nothing left to give. It's the pain threshold, but I call it the disappointment threshold, because nothing disappoints you more than being a jockey. You get beaten all the time, even if you're good, and it empties you all the time until the tank's so empty you can't fill it up again.'

What jockeys go through hasn't changed; the most recent stats from the Injured Jockeys Fund show the median age a jump jockey retires is 31, they have an average of 16 rides per fall, one injury in 83 rides, and 18 per cent of falls result in injury, with 215 rides a year. (Flat jockeys have on average, one injury in 594 rides and 240 rides per fall.)

* * *

See You did everything that the rightly celebrated three-time Champion Hurdler Istabraq did. As Corky says, 'The way he came to the last, as long as he wasn't in front too long, he'd go up that hill in better time than Istabraq,' but the public never got to know him. 'No one knew who he was, or his owners,' Nicky says, 'We ran him once a year, any other way and we'd never have got to Cheltenham. It was a plan, with Frank, that worked.'

He was just the fourth horse to win three consecutive Champion Hurdles, after Hatton's Grace, in 1949-51, a pint-sized horse who came into his own in the hands of the legendary trainer Vincent O'Brien. Then, Sir Ken in 1952-54, a horse with a temper so wicked he fought his field companion to the death. And Persian War in 1968-70, a good-natured maniac who once lost two teeth hitting a hurdle, and whose heart is buried at Genesis Green Stud in Newmarket where he lived out his days. Istabraq, sired by Sadler's Wells, trained by Aidan O'Brien and owned by JP McManus, was the fifth in 1998-2000, and only denied a chance for his fourth title when the foot and mouth epidemic closed the Festival. No other horse – or trainer – has since managed to pull off such a coup.

Even when See You was brutish, he wasn't stupid and he never picked a battle he couldn't win. 'When we turned him out with others, they bullied him!' Nicky says, 'I went to see him at Stype Farm Stud, and he looked awful, scars all over him, the other horses were biting him and bullying him!' Nicky wasn't having his Champion hurdler being humiliated so he got him a donkey and he became king again. 'It was only a donkey that wouldn't chase him,' he says. 'They always say the best horse will stand on the high ground and for evermore, he was always on the top of the hill where the king will stand.'

4

REMITTANCE MAN

The Champion chaser and born worrier who found peace with Nobby the sheep

THE HEART wants what it wants, and when Nicky saw Remittance Man at the Irish Derby Sales in Dublin, he was immediately smitten and followed his feeling against all reason: 'I fell in love with him. Nobody else could have done; everything was wrong. He was small, narrow, lean, but I'd never seen a horse that moved like him.'

Nicky was, as always, accompanied by his long-time friend and collaborator, the bloodstock agent, David Minton, known throughout the racing world as Minty. He is the agent supreme and has worked with Nicky since he set up in 1978 and they were good friends before that. Minty says, 'He's an incredible man, with extraordinary patience, and he loves a party; I don't know where he gets his energy from.' When it comes to the horses, they are instinctively in tune. Minty says they have 'the same eye for a horse, I know what he wants and he knows what I like'.

'There are a million things you look for,' Nicky explains. 'If it's walking with a good swing, the tail will swing, they'll use themselves properly. They've got to be natural athletes. You've got an individual horse, and it walks by, and it's by so-and-so, and you decide you like it. No one has ever sat on them, so we know nothing, and every now and then after six months, you think, this one can go. You need an enormously good team for feedback, riding every day and looking after them. Here everyone looks after three horses each and are seriously married to them and the guys can tell me – the margin is tiny – this doesn't feel quite right.'

Minty and Nicky both wanted this horse. Minty remembers, 'He was lean, leggy, and he walked better than anything you've seen – a long, active stride, his hind foot landed in front of his fore. It was poetry in motion.' He was theirs for £18,000. He wasn't the first good horse they had bought (that was First Bout) but he was the first great one.

The horse was sent to Henrietta Knight at West Lockinge Farm, where Caroline Gordon broke him in. She saw at once he was 'very nicely put together; Minty knows what he's buying,' and he was only with her for a few months because he was so uncomplicated. She long-reined him, rode him round the roads with the older horses, a little canter here and there, and once a week took him to the loose jumping school to let him learn how to jump and 'straightaway it was so natural for him'. She remembers he was 'a complete athlete, it all happened very easily, his breath was always regular, he wasn't anxious, all that makes it economical in a race if they can relax and breathe properly, it's all the little things you put together for the complete article'.

He made an impression, as horses are wont to do, and all these decades on, Caroline remembers that he was 'a bit of an introvert, he was thinking too hard about life. He was a quiet soul, he wasn't a huge in-your-face character, straightforward as long as everything was in place, if not he obviously worried about things.'

She says, 'I used to love doing the three-, four- and five-year-olds, you can make your own assessment, without telling anyone, and then see if you're right or wrong.' When Nicky asked for her opinion, as he always did, she told him he was a 'lovely horse, an athlete, jumps for fun, it was all very easy for him. He had the scope to jump big and the right attitude, he never worried about it, he knew how to place his feet, never looked hesitant, he was intelligent. The key was to keep him relaxed in his stable, eating properly.'

* * *

When he returned to Nicky's yard, Iain Major took on this 'proper quirky' horse. He says, 'We all thought he had an engine, but he was a bit crackers.' He went to great lengths to soothe him; in the afternoons he'd put a space hopper into the stable or sit in his manger and sing to him; anything to take his mind off whatever was vexing him. And every night, he'd take his dog out at about 10pm, walking from the village down to the yard. He remembers, 'I opened the door to the yard and he'd be waiting for me every single night. Everything else would be asleep, he was the only one, he knew his old man was coming to give him carrots and once he'd had them, he'd settle down.'

* * *

Nicky had three horses to show the late John Collins. He was always known as Tim from his Royal Navy nickname Tiny Tim (he was 6ft 6in tall) and after that, the Commander, after he won bricks of cash playing roulette in a casino at Le Touquet in the 1940s. One flamboyant gesture deserves another so, all in good time, he invested his winnings in racehorses. He told Nicky he wanted a three-year-old so he could enjoy following the horse through its career. He saw the Man, and said, 'I like the look in his eye,' remembers his widow, Jenny. 'His very good walk might have been a reason but it was the look in his eye!' Sired by Prince Regent out of the dam, Mittens I, Remittance Man was named.

Tim had a significant hand in saving Cheltenham from property developers, setting up the Racecourse Holdings Trust with Nicky's father Johnny. He was given free entry for life and Nicky was Tim's first wife's godson (the links in racing are interlocked like plaits in a mane). There was warmth in those connections. Tim and Jenny watched the gallops regularly and 'we always thought he was perfectly marvellous,' Jenny remembers. 'We would have thought that, even if he wasn't. We were very excited by him, he moved beautifully at any pace.'

Minty says, 'We thought we'd done a very good job,' but after two years, Nicky could only muster two wins over hurdles, and was at such a loss, he even tried him over three miles. He was endlessly placed, but 'there was always a reason, he was running quite well and was just beaten,' says Jenny.

By chance he jumped a fence at Windsor House and Nicky remembers, 'he was electric …: brilliant, he could do things I'd never seen horses do'. He was the first of just three horses in Nicky's career that, when he first schooled them over fences, he realised they'd found something very special. His jockey Richard Dunwoody agrees, 'The first time he schooled in Lambourn, he shone, he was fantastic. Usually, you spend the first morning going over the baby fences to get confident, then the babies again, then the bigger ones, but that first morning we sent him straight over the bigger fences.' Nicky had found the key. Or, rather, one of them (there would be two).

* * *

Jamie Osborne was Nicky's amateur-turned-conditional jockey, and ranks himself as 'probably his worst' stable lad (Nicky says he's a great horseman). The yard was run 'almost like a little horsey army camp', but with a queue of people wanting to work in Lambourn's best yards, he knew he was in a privileged position.

'In those days, I found Nicky uptight and on edge all the time; he's very different now, he's completely mellowed.' He was, in Jamie's eyes, 'a man in a hurry, very determined, eager for everything to run smoothly, nothing to go wrong, and still the same today. He's a hungry animal, it probably manifested itself differently in those days than now, when he's got years and years of experience, it probably sits more comfortably with him.'

Jamie was learning what it would take to be a great jockey. 'Ability and mental strength are probably equally important,' he says, 'you're going to get knocks, physically and mentally, and if you can't cope with that, you won't last. It's a sport where you compete several times a day, most days of the week, unlike others where you build up for an event, compete and then go back to training. It's unique, and serious mental resilience and consistency is key.'

And then, there are the injuries. 'You knew you were going to get hurt and the huge fear, if you had time off through injury, was that other people would take your place and your rides would become their rides. There was a lot of pressure to minimise the length of time injuries took.' Letting jockeys decide when they are ready to return from injury is like asking a Labrador to supervise the larder. Jamie remembers a bad injury towards the end of his career, 'brought about by the fact that I was riding with a broken collarbone' and as he fell, on the other side, he tried to save himself, landed on his left side and smashed his wrist (though he saved his right collarbone!).

* * *

Jockeys are a breed apart. Charlie Mann, for example, broke his neck in a racing accident in 1989 and it finished his career as he was refused a jockey licence. 'When you're a jockey and you're riding, you don't want to do anything else.' He was 32 when he was forced into retirement, and he couldn't get the decision overturned.

'We live to ride,' he says, 'I didn't think any further than that, you don't think what you will do when you pack up because you don't want to pack up and when you get stopped, it's devastating, worse than a death.' Sports psychologist Michael Caulfield says that elite sportsmen and women are 'the only people that die twice; their life is consumed in thrilling activity and when they stop, they're immediately spoken of in the past tense'.

Charlie had started riding out in Newmarket when 'we didn't have helmets, you turned your cap around' and jockeys didn't have to wear back protectors so he didn't. He remembers a hurdle race at Kempton, 'I was quite cocky when I was young, and in a race, the top guy goes down the inside, you don't start going up their inner, there's a pecking order. I went up the inside and another jockey grabbed my bridle by the browband. All of a sudden, I had no bridle.' He's also been through the wing a few times, 'because you shouldn't be where you didn't have the right to be. You learn.'

Having lost his licence, Charlie felt he had unfinished business in the saddle, and was determined to find a way around his ban. Six years after he broke his neck, he had his biggest win. He forged a licence from something batty he'd found on the internet, had a bold horse with a big jump, and lined up (for the second time) in the 1995 Czech Grand National.

The Velká Pardubická is the oldest and most deranged steeplechase in the world and has been since its inaugural run in 1874. It's four-and-a-bit miles, 31 fences, and involves about a mile through a ploughed field, ('it's tradition, there's no reason why it should be ploughed'), a nearly 10ft long water jump, the Taxi (a 5ft hedge, 16ft ditch, and about 32ft wide from take-off to landing 'with a graveyard next to it') a wall, a bank to shimmy up and down, and the French where two hedges are jumped as one. Never have all the horses that started the race finished it. Charlie's mount was It's a Snip who may have been 'slow as a hearse' on British turf, but here he came into his own. Charlie kept him till the end of his days, and still admires how game and sweet he was.

* * *

As Nicky's amateur, Jamie did as he was told. He was beaten in a race and Nicky had specifically told him how to ride it. In those days, racing wasn't on television, so if trainers weren't at the race, they couldn't watch. 'He had told me not to hit the front before the second and the newspapers said I took it up three out,' he says. In fact, 'I didn't actually' but when he said that, Nicky wasn't having it. 'He said, "You must have done! It says so in the paper!" He got really annoyed and threw a phone at me.' It could have been worse; trainer Jenny Pitman once surprised Jamie with a left hook. A horse had gone out through the rails at the Scottish National and 'she thought it was my fault and she wanted to police the situation herself. I wasn't expecting it at all.'

He remembers Remittance Man as a 'pretty insignificant looking horse, not the scopey, beautiful, quality horses that Nicky used to buy. If 20 horses arrived at the yard, in physical attributes and quality he'd have been 20 of 20. He was wiry, a bit narrow, a bit plain, but when you rode him, he had a beautiful way of going, very well-balanced and fluid. He kept getting beaten in novice hurdles, confirming everyone's suspicion he wasn't much good. No one dreamed he'd reach the heights that he did.'

Jamie left to work for Oliver Sherwood, and his parents later wrote to Nicky, thanking him for being so good to him (Nicky still has the letter). Now a trainer himself, what Jamie took from those days was, 'Nicky's total dedication, he's relentless, a machine, and his enthusiasm never wanes. Even now if a horse gets beat, it hurts. There is nothing blasé about him, he wouldn't take anything for granted and he's as hungry as he always was.' As Nicky says, 'If you have no competitive spirit, it's pointless. You're not taking part to come second.'

* * *

Remittance Man had made his intentions clear and November 1990 was a breeze, marking the start of a long, shimmering run of glory. Everything he touched, with one exception, turned to gold for 14 races. With Richard Dunwoody on board, the pair racked up seven straight victories, including the two-mile-four-furlong Hopeful Chase at Newbury by 30 lengths, the Grade Two Novices' Chase at Kempton in February 1991 by the same margin, the Grade One Arkle Challenge Trophy at Cheltenham beating Uncle Ernie by six lengths the next month ('he stayed on well up the hill, it was an open race going into it, he gave me some ride,' remembers Richard), and the Arlington Premier Series Steeple Chase Final back at Newbury in February 1992, beating Captain Dibble by 20 lengths. 'He was a straightforward ride,' Richard says, 'but went well clear from the fourth fence. Horses can lose concentration and get lonely at the front for too long. Jockeys can get it wrong as well. It puts the pressure on if you make a stupid mistake, you're pretty exposed.' Jenny was thrilled, 'Richard was not an extrovert, but extremely nice and whatever he said was very good sense. You knew perfectly well he'd produce the best the horse could give; he was a brilliant horseman.'

Iain Major took to riding Remittance Man at home, once the yard had moved to Seven Barrows and says his behaviour was always flawless. He remembers one of his first gallops, 'He strung them out like the washing! All the good horses were behind. I said I'd lead, and we hacked up there. They all swore at me for going too quick. He would do one bit of work, and once he'd done that, he'd got himself fit, and the rest of the time he was useless. He got himself fit and then stopped – he was far brighter than the lot of us.'

Iain just loved him. 'God yes, he was my life for a while, you dream of getting a horse like that. I used to spend that much time with him, he was my mate really.' Remittance Man's smarts meant that 'when he was ready for a big race, and he got really fit, he was appalling, you couldn't get near him. You had to be very careful. The night before the Arkle or Champion Chase, he bit me on both my shoulders and I said, he's ready, he's not in a good mood, and afterwards, he'd calm down again. Like a fighter when they're ready to go – it was the only time he ever did that, he was a lamb most of the time.'

The unbroken run hit a bump in December 1991 when Jamie was back on board (because Richard Dunwoody was on the people's champion Desert Orchid, a faller in what would be his last race), for the three-mile Grade One King George Chase at Kempton. He was third by just three-and-a-half lengths. Close, but to a sportsman, when there's only one position of interest, he may as well have been last. Even now, his regret as fresh as if the race was yesterday, Jamie says, 'I went too soon! I don't think I rode him very well. He was in front upsides at the second last and petered out a little bit. If I'd ridden him a bit colder, in a more conservative way, I'd have got closer to The Fellow.' Nicky responds, 'I won't disagree, but I never said it. I never criticise jockeys on the other side of the saddling enclosure. We might talk about it, it can be bubbling under, you could be hopping mad if they've done something really stupid but you trust your jockey to have a Plan A, B, C, D and to use their brains. The plan invariably has to change and we'll discuss it afterwards.'

* * *

John Francome says a good jockey should return to the ring and know that this horse needs a left-handed track, or three miles, anything that can help the trainer continue to compile the composite picture. John's mentor was Richard Pitman, who strode into the ring, cheerful and chatty. 'For most people you could insult their kids before you insult their horse,' John says. 'Be careful what you say, it's a big part of being a jockey, making people feel at ease. If they think you're nervous they'll be nervous, then the horse will be too.' He remembers one jockey, on a slow horse, who came back and said to the great amusement of his fellow lads, 'This horse will never win a race until it's inside a greyhound.' He never rode for the owner or the trainer again.

Mick Fitzgerald now coaches young jockeys and says, 'Riding is very often the easy part, I tell them that you have to be the whole package, it's not about the riding, it's about walking into the paddock and giving the owners their money's worth when you ride. They can choose and it costs the same to have Frankie Dettori as to have a jockey who has never ridden a winner, so why choose them when you can have Frankie?'

Generally, the stable jockey makes the best jockey because he knows his horse inside out. After the race, 'I don't want an excuse,' Nicky says, 'I want to believe him: he doesn't like soft ground, he can't breathe, tell me anything constructive. Don't think of the first excuse that comes into your head. The problem with an inexperienced rider is by the time they're back they've dreamt up an amazing synopsis and blamed it on something. I file that in the bin.' Mick adds that while it's usually the best idea to know the horse, 'Sometimes it can pay to have someone who's never ridden the horse before because you're not hanging on to an old memory. If you drive a car, you always remember how it was the first time you drove it, you expect that feel every time, if you're fresh you don't have that history.'

Richard remembers getting no more detailed instructions than 'you know what to do, kick on from the second last, try not to overcomplicate, try to get the lead over the last'. And no post-race analysis either; they both knew if something hadn't gone right.

* * *

Come the Grade One Queen Mother Champion Chase, on 11 March at the 1992 Cheltenham Festival, Richard was on Waterloo Boy, for the trainer David Nicholls, so Jamie was back with the Man. 'I was on a high, I'd had the treble on day one and I remember thinking I'd used up all my luck for the week, riding three winners the day before.' Still, he knew the horse, with the 'good cruising speed, straightforward, neat in front of a fence, knew where his feet were, tremendous scope, but no turbo booster, very fluent over fences', and it was his job to get him 'close to top gear, keep him as fluid as possible and pray that was enough to burn off the opposition'. Luck and a prayer. When did he think he'd win? 'Never, there's always another bloody fence coming up.' When they beat Katabatic by a length, it was Nicky's first Champion Chase, the most prestigious two-mile chase of the season. Richard rolled in third and took it as gallantly as any jockey would. 'It was particularly galling when Jamie came screaming past me … that's the way it goes … I hope I congratulated him … maybe.'

Richard's competitive edge was so fierce it blinded him. Jamie says he never competed with him without learning something new and AP says now how deeply he always admired Richard. 'He was very stubborn, selfish, single-minded, focused, and mentally and physically unbelievably tough. I saw that if I wanted to be champion, I had to keep getting up, even when I didn't feel I could. I had no interest in anyone else in sport or business or any walk of life, his madness was what made him the best.'

Richard responds, 'That's what it was like then. Selfish? Totally. Self-absorbed and whatever else it took at the time.' When he and Adrian Maguire were neck-and-neck to be champion jockey, towards the end of the 1991/92 season, both of them barely missed a day. They would ride around 900 races a year, walking away from 60 to 70 falls. After every single one, 'We were in bits but mentally we kept going,' he recalls. 'That's how it was, that's what it required. I needed to be on top of everything all the time to get there and if I'd given one inch, Adrian would have beaten me.'

He was eaten up with the competition, obsessed, and Michael Caulfield, then head of the Professional Jockeys Association (now a sports psychologist) watched him climbing the walls as Adrian went 50 winners clear of him by Christmas and suggested Richard talk to a sports psychologist. Michael says, for Richard, his desire to win was 'his greatest strength and biggest weakness. He couldn't cope with not winning every day and horse-racing is a losing sport; unless you're absolutely remarkable you'll get beaten on 85 per cent of your rides.' He saw Richard put himself through 'daily purgatory, he saw it as part of the process, he wasn't happy unless he was under that degree of pressure'. That's just how it is at the elite level. 'They are different,' Michael says, 'they are not like you or me or 99.9 per cent of the population. I admire them for wanting to put their bodies and minds through utter hell, they are brothers and sisters in arms, and they've taught me so much about human behaviour and madness and the absolute desire to be better at what they do.'

Not everyone reacted that way; when the tabloids got wind of Richard's visit to the sports psychologist, they splashed with 'DunMADDY' headlines. 'I was totally losing the mental battle, I was really struggling,' Richard says now. What did the psychologist make him see? 'You have to focus on what you can control. The main thing is, stick to your own job, worry about your own horse, think of getting the best out of them. It helped massively.' How out of control was he? 'I was too focused on worrying about what Adrian was doing in a race which led to me running him out through the rails at Nottingham in the season we were going for the Championship.' He was, as he knew he would be, suspended for 14 days and missed Cheltenham – the Olympics of the racing world – for the offence.

Jenny Collins remembers he'd been warned off for doing 'something frightful, and it was inconvenient when he was banned'. Mick Fitzgerald took the ride on favourite Remittance Man in the 1994 Queen Mother Champion Chase. He says ruefully that his memory is 'watching him gallop off into the distance when I put him on the deck. He was a gent, a lovely horse, and it was a golden opportunity for me when I rode him in that race and I made a novice mistake, I fully hold my hands up, sometimes you get it wrong and it was one of those days.'

* * *

Mick had arrived at Nicky's yard as a 22-year-old champion apprentice in 1993 and remembers 'the first year was a little bit tricky, finding my feet, not sure if I'll fit into the mould. One thing you realise with Nicky, he goes above and beyond with people around him to make them feel comfortable. He organised for me to see Terry Biddlecombe and Yogi Bresner to help me with my riding.' (Terry went on to train Best Mate with his wife Henrietta Knight to win three consecutive Gold Cups and Yogi is the world-class jumps coach.) 'He really wanted it to work,' Mick says, 'which meant an awful lot. Having a trainer with that much confidence in you is a big deal, and if you feel that from them, it makes you not doubt yourself and that's huge, because riding is all about confidence. Every jockey at some stage in their career will doubt themselves, but if you've got a trainer that never gives the impression they're doubting you, you get over it very quickly. A trainer doubting a jockey and the jockey doubting themselves is not a good recipe. You're not human unless you do; you're only as good as your last winner. Many would say it was cocky; I was confident in my own ability, I always thought I was the best rider. I admit when I look back, I shake my head, I was deluded but I believed it – you have to – and having someone like Nicky at your shoulder is a huge deal. We were together for 15 years, never a cross word, I was always honest with him and he always made me think I was riding to the top of my ability.'

As Michael Caulfield says, racing is a losing sport. And Mick, with all of his winners, including nearly 70 for Nicky at the very highest level like the RSA Chase and Hennessy Gold Cup on Trabolgan, the Novices' Hurdle at Kempton on Binocular, the Punchestown Champion Hurdle on Punjabi, says, 'So many other things go against you – even as a jockey if you're operating at a 20 per cent strike rate, which is pretty good, that means you're getting beat on four before you win on the fifth.' What Mick learned from watching Nicky was that 'he's a great loser. As well as a great winner, but you lose more than you win. I was never a great loser, I learned to be a bit better, to lose with a bit of class, something I wasn't capable of when I started, I learned over time. He's a gentleman, he really is.'

Mick says one of Nicky's great skills is that he's a 'great race watcher and a great race reader, he can see what's happening in a race whereas some aren't as good at reading a race or how well a horse is travelling or why you did a certain thing in a race. That's why he's always liked having a stable jockey, he's not guessing what that jockey is doing, he knows how they ride and he can see by their body language how the race is going.' Mick knew Nicky's mood from the moment he walked into the covered ride and says he's the man for his ability to get a horse ready for the big day: 'It's always been his biggest selling point, if you've got a horse that's good enough, you know he's going to have it ready.'

* * *

Having swept the board, for two full years, from the Hopeful Chase, the Arlington Qualifier and the Arlington Final at Newbury, to the Novices' Chase at Ascot, two Novices' Chases, the King George and the Emblem Chase at Kempton, the Arkle and the Champion Chase at Cheltenham and the Melling Chase at Aintree, and after his fall at Cheltenham in the Champion Chase in 1994, there were just two more races for the Man – fourth in both – and he retired.

All of this – the 13 wins from 17 runs over fences, favourite in 15 of those, earnings of £267,093 – might never have happened. Nicky's love at first sight for this horse had been stress-tested when it was immediately obvious that he was a box-walker, par excellence, endlessly lapping his stable. It's one of the behavioural vices, along with crib-biting or wind sucking when a horse clamps its teeth to a post, or the top of a stable door and gulps air, that are considered such bad habits that, if undeclared, mean the horse can be returned. 'It's a horrendous habit and I should have sent him back,' Nicky admits, with no regret at all, but the heart wants what it wants and all that, so he kept the faith.

But in the meantime, how to stop the box-walking? A succession of single sheep borrowed from his father's farm arrived to do a season – like debutants – to keep the horse company. Ridley Lamb (named after the jockey who won the Gold Cup in a blizzard) was followed by Allan Lamb (after the England cricketer) then Nobby. When Nobby's replacement arrived, Remittance Man had already decided he wanted Nobby back, and the replacement had no time to even introduce himself before he was chucked over the door by the Man. Twice. He didn't even stay long enough to be given a name.

Nobby had to be found. 'Where is he?' Nicky asked his father. 'There are 400 in that field and he's one of them,' hardly narrowed it down. What to do? How to find the needle in the haystack? 'We rode a horse into the field, 399 went the other way and Nobby came out.'

They were reunited, Nobby was his 'constant companion', pacing the yard when the Man was on the gallops, accompanying him to the racecourse for overnighters and retiring with him. To Gemma Pearson, equine behaviourist and vet, 'it makes perfect sense, it's an individual personality, the same as we form a friendship with another'. She calls it the 'survival of the friendliest'; sheep and horses are both herd animals and prey and 'if they're happy to be in each other's company, from an evolutionary point of view, it gives them an advantage in terms of survival'.

Remittance Man and Nobby spent their summer holidays with the family Collins. 'One terrible time we didn't think we'd have Nobby,' remembers Jenny, 'We had sheep in the field so there was no point. Nicky turned Nobby out with his father's sheep and when someone led the horses down the road, Nobby saw them, said, "I'm not a sheep," got out under the rails and joined them. Remittance Man went round the field looking for Nobby, didn't find him, so got another one by the scruff of its neck and shook it!'

* * *

Remittance Man isn't the first horse to choose the company he keeps from a different gene pool. Godolphin Arabian (1724-1753) is one of the three thoroughbreds from which every single racehorse is descended and saved all his love for a cat called Grimalkin. When the cat died, he rejected all replacements. Don't Push It, the horse that gave AP McCoy his first Grand National win in 2010, didn't enjoy the company of other horses, nor being alone. He found peace with a sheep and at one point had his own flock of six. Foinavon, the 100/1 outsider for the 1967 Grand National, which he won by being so far behind the pack that he missed the pile up at the 23rd fence, lived with a goat called Susie. Goats and horses have such a long-standing history that the expression to 'get your goat' comes from competitors stealing a goat from a horse's stable the night before a race to unsettle the horse.

* * *

When Remittance Man retired, Nobby accompanied him to the Collinses'. Jenny commissioned a limited edition bronze of the two in a field from the sculptor Philip Blacker. He remembers being pleased he got a good physical likeness and including Nobby in the piece meant he could bring out the personality of the horse, and create the connection 'which was obviously there'. He says, 'It was obvious they were inseparable; one doesn't want to anthropomorphise but there was a great attachment to each other.' In the sculpture, the horse's elegant neck is curled, he is looking intently at Nobby, but Nobby is looking elsewhere. 'I got the feeling it was a slightly one-sided relationship, he liked Nobby more than Nobby liked him,' Philip says.

Still, no one liked Remittance Man more than Iain Major, who retired from racing at the same time as him, and who still lives in Lambourn. He says, 'I travel that road to the gallops on my bike or driving and on nice sunny days, it's very rare that I don't remember him. It was one of those moments in time, he was the best two-mile chaser in the world. It was a joy.'

5

CARACCIOLA

The oldest Royal Ascot winner ever, always game and unconventional

WHEN CARACCIOLA'S new owner, Piers Pottinger, met him for the first time at Seven Barrows in 2002, there was an immediate bond, and an unspoken promise. He remembers, 'He gave me a nudge with his head: OK mate, we're on, we're going to have some fun.' It felt as though he'd been chosen. He adds, 'There was something about him. He was different. He wasn't particularly big, but he was good-looking and he had this character.'

The horse kept his word, throughout his eight-year, 51-race career. Mick Fitzgerald partnered him regularly for the first six years of it and describes him as 'an absolute gent, a lovely, bonny horse, a nice person to be around, very straightforward, and a real trier'.

They won two Novices' Hurdles early on at Newbury and Sandown, and a Novices' Chase at Kempton. Mick remembers, 'He dug deep that day, I was very proud of him, he was brave,' but he didn't win another run over fences. Looking back on it now, Mick says, 'He wasn't really a chaser, he was a little bit timid, he had a lot of speed, I always felt the jumping took plenty out of him, he was a better flat horse. He had plenty of runs, I just never felt he was a natural chaser. He always tried to jump too clean, it was hard work for him. He wasn't overly big. He was a good jumper, but he was too good, too safe. It takes too much out of them sometimes, they put so much effort into jumping when it comes to racing, there's not enough left in the tank.'

Back he would go to hurdles; jockey Andrew Tinkler remembers landing a fourth place when Caracciola was ten, in the 20-runner Trophy Hurdle handicap at Newbury in 2007. He says, 'He was very easy to ride, and that's a really rough race. You need to travel and jump solidly, in a big field it counts for so much because you can get into the gaps when you need to, and he gave me a dream ride. He did all the things he needed to, we were there at the business end with every chance and got run out of it but he gave me a super ride.' For Andrew it wasn't just that he was 'neat, accurate with his feet and springy' but it was his character. 'He was mentally tough,' he says, 'he could hold his own in any race and those big fields have horses with extreme talent. If the horse hasn't got the mindset to cope with it – a big field and a rough race – it doesn't matter about the talent, he won't come out the other side successful. He never lacked in heart and willingness.'

Nicky had bought this well-bred five-year-old for jumping, and says, 'German horses have amazing pedigrees, we like them a lot, they're very tough, very strong, very good families,' but, as Piers says, 'It's fair to say he never quite did what we expected over hurdles and fences.' He was game, and talented, and Piers wasn't expecting any miracles; he's owned horses for long enough to know that plenty of owners never win a single race. He was one of those himself for a while. He says, 'You learn patience in racing. I'm not naturally patient, and you learn to take the rough with the smooth, which includes once being written up as the unluckiest owner, as I'd gone 14 years without a win. Out of the blue I got a letter from Peter O'Sullevan saying, "You've got two years to go to equal me, I was 16 years an owner before I won."'

A flash of inspiration was needed, and Nicky had a highly unusual idea. 'Suddenly I thought, let's give him a run on the flat, it just occurred to me, I don't know why.' It was unheard of, in effect to reverse the traditional order of a horse's career, most don't get faster as they get older.

The physiological development of racehorses is completed between four and five years old. A study in the *Journal of Equine Science* about the effect of age on a racehorse's performance on the flat found that usually the rate that the horse improves from two to four-and-a-half years old is a steeper incline than the rate of decline after that age. In flat racing, a typical horse improves by ten lengths in a sprint (under one mile) and 15 lengths (over a mile) from age two to four-and-a-half. Over the next five years, the typical horse declines by six lengths for sprints and nine-and-a-half for longer. Caracciola was anything but typical, and Nicky's decision wasn't entirely random, as he explains, 'He was so versatile, a very, very good hurdler, but he wasn't really big enough to be a top-class chaser, he didn't have the scope for it, so he came back to hurdling, but he was so high in the handicaps he couldn't win, so we went flat racing.'

Piers says, 'I'll never forget it, Nicky said, "I think we should try running him on the flat again, he was a proven winner on the flat before we bought him."' The exchange sums up why Piers found so much pleasure in being an owner with a horse in training with Nicky. He explains, 'He's a fantastic communicator, he was meticulous, we discussed it and I felt properly involved. He's a trainer of immense stature, I don't know any other trainer in his league. I leave it to the pros to make the real decisions but it's nice to feel involved and have an explanation as an owner. You always want to go to the great races; it was only through owning horses for a while I understood the reality and realistic prospects.' So, Piers said, 'Great, let's do it', adding, 'We weren't expecting anything but he won and off we went.'

When the ten-year-old Caracciola lined up at Bath, for a two-mile-one-furlong handicap, it was his 34th start for Nicky (in National Hunt racing, horses race on average seven times a year), and his jockey Eddie Ahern already knew him, as a 'big, loveable, gentle giant' and says, 'Once you get that bond with a horse they'll do anything for you. In a tight finish, they'll get their head down and stretch for you. That's why it's so important for trainers to find the right jockey on the right horse on the right day; there's so much that's goes into training horses, not just getting the horse fit; it's the right race, right course, and I was definitely the right jockey for him.' He adds that so much of what he does is instinctive, intuitive, and can't be taught, but 'as a jockey you don't know you're doing it, the way you ride, the way you talk to the horse, the way you pat them on the neck and reassure them, the horses begin to like certain people and I think Caracciola liked me'.

* * *

Caracciola had found his place and, with Eddie, went on to be second in the Cesarewitch at Newmarket in 2007 in a vast field of 33, narrowly beaten by the six-year-old Leg Spinner. It's a race that Nicky had won in 2003 with Landing Light and Pat Eddery and would go on to win with Buzz and Oisin Murphy in 2021. Caracciola and Eddie returned the next year, at odds of 50/1 and the horse now aged 11, racing against three-to-six-year-olds. Piers was a little affronted by the price, 'I asked Eddie, why on earth, in A1 condition, tip top form would he be 50/1 and he said, "It's just his age, they think he's too old."' They were wrong.

Eddie remembers the joy of it all, 'It was an amazing day. Big handicap fields with lots of runners over a long distance are very difficult to win. He loved long trips and he outstayed everything.' He knew how Caracciola liked to race, so 'when I rode him, I'd get him into mid division, going easy, he was always taking a pull, I'd be saying, don't go yet, don't go yet'. He says now, 'To have a horse that age, to race at that level and win, coming off a hurdling and chasing career? His staying power was massive, his stamina was unbelievable,' and as the two-mile-two-furlong race spread out, he could see 'horses were getting tired around me, not going, he was the only one who was getting going.'

In a field of 32 runners, the pair saw off the three-year-old favourite, Askar Tau (fourth), Ryan Moore and four-year-old Mamlook, who came in third and Arc Bleu with Johnny Murtagh in second place. He was the oldest by at least four years and only two horses carried more weight than he did. Mick says of this new direction, 'It was almost a relief when he was running on the flat, he didn't have to work so hard.'

When Caracciola beat the favourite, five-year-old Friston Forest in the one-mile-six-furlong Grand Cup at York, he set another record by being the oldest horse to win a Listed race, aged 12. (Listed races are a step below Group races. The five Classics – the Oaks and the Derby at Epsom, the 1,000 Guineas and the 2,000 Guineas at Newmarket, and the St Leger at Doncaster – are the most prestigious of all Group Ones, followed by Group Two and Three.)

Eddie wasn't available and Piers suggested Dale Gibson instead. He was at that time the oldest northern jockey, and when he retired a month later, 'he said Caracciola was his most enjoyable ride and he wrote me a letter thanking me for it,' Piers remembers. Something special was in the air.

* * *

Eddie can't remember a time in his life without horses; they sent their cue early on. His first memories are of wanting to see them, trying to climb out of a baby-chair, or the backseat of a car whenever he heard them trotting down the road. He was always happiest 'standing at the gate, feeding them grass, trying to get them eating out of my hand'. Years on, he describes himself as a horseman, and says that while 'there are plenty of good jockeys, they're not horsemen'. Plenty of horsemen aren't jockeys, but those that are, as Eddie explains, will always be 'concerned about the horse's welfare, how the horse is feeling, how to talk to him if he's sweating or jig-jogging, how to calm him down, make him feel good, and reassure him. I like to think I was able to do that with the horses I rode. A horse can't talk but he gives you a signal and signs a horseman can read that other people can't.'

Being a horseman is still a gift so rare and special, it's a shorthand for an entire way of being. Mick says a horseman is 'somebody who sees beyond the glaringly obvious, if you are a man or woman and you have an ability to connect with a horse, you're a horseman or woman'.

Eddie remembers the instant link, 'Often I cantered a horse to the start and they gave me such a good feeling, I was thinking this horse is going to win today. Super form, bouncing, I love everything about him. Listening to his breathing, watching his muscles on his shoulder, feeling his legs float over the ground, watching his ears pricked and his eyes gazing; you just love them straight away. Sometimes you can love them without getting on, you see one and think, he's amazing and you're looking forward to getting on, I can't wait to ride him, you fall in love straight away.'

* * *

The friendship between Piers and Nicky goes back years and they share two traits that are both welcomed in racing. One is a passion. 'He gets quite emotional,' Piers says, 'as I do, when we're together it can get a bit emotional, he wears his heart on his sleeve.' And the other is being highly superstitious; racing is full of irrational beliefs. One jockey used to trample new silks on the floor before putting them on; another carries two whips in his bag, but one has never been used; another refuses to be first jockey in the paddock if he's riding a favourite; Frankie Dettori always has a strip of white tape on his stirrup, since the first time he tried it and won the Derby in 2007. Green is unilaterally unlucky: when Piers dressed in the wrong colour at the races early on, he remembers 'Nicky told me, "You shouldn't be wearing a green suit on a racecourse," and I never have since then.' Another time, readying for the traditional 'serious' lunch at The Pheasant in Lambourn on the Monday before Cheltenham, Piers remembers, 'Johnny the Fish was an owner and also landlord of the pub, he told me that he'd been to the pub before lunch to drop something off and he was worried that there would be "13 for lunch and Nicky won't have 13 sitting down at a table". "No of course, obviously not, and neither will I. What are we going to do?"' Piers asked Johnny the Fish if he could join them but he was too busy. So, they came up with a solution, and walked through the pub asking, does anyone want lunch? 'And someone put their hand up and joined us!'

So it was, a month after his York triumph, 12-year-old Caracciola was ready for the prestige of Royal Ascot and the two-mile-five-and-a-half-furlong Queen Alexandra Stakes, Britain's longest flat race. Nicky called Piers and as he recalls, 'Nicky said he was fishing in Scotland but he was coming down for this, and I said, "No, you're not." "What do you mean, no I'm not?" I said, "Every time you turn up he doesn't win, when you're not there, he wins." "Fair enough," he said, "I'm banned."'

Piers' entire family arrived instead, including two of his children who had flown in from Australia just to see the race and arrived that morning. Eddie remembers how much Caracciola enjoyed it, 'He loved the big occasion, he could feel the atmosphere of Royal Ascot, he'd come alive. In the parade ring, the head comes up, the chest comes out, they look taller and wider. He loved it and the bigger the race the better.' For Eddie, a horse so willing made every minute a pleasure. 'Good horses like him are so easy to ride,' he says, 'you always found yourself in a good position, if anything was going wrong in a race you could shuffle back, or if you got pushed wide, you were always able to get back into the position you want to be in. You need a good engine.'

Come the race, he remembers it as though he has just hopped off the horse in the winner's enclosure, 'I was biding my time, saying, wait, wait, wait, everyone was coming off the bridle, jockeys were getting down and pushing, I was sitting down thinking, oh my God, I'm going to win this. At three and four furlongs, everyone's getting tired and he's coming into himself. I definitely knew I had it in the bag at the two-furlong point. It's like he looks over at everybody and says "hey guys you're all stopping and I'm only getting going".'

It was a record-breaking win; he was the oldest horse by two years to win the race. The next three horses home were all four-year-olds and carrying seven pounds less and it wasn't a slow year. There were no special circumstances. His winning time of 4.53.89 minutes was almost exactly the same as Cover Up, a five-year-old ridden by Kieren Fallon and trained by Sir Michael Stoute in 2002, and Romany Rue, a four-year-old ridden by the late Walter Swinburn (Shergar's jockey) and trained by Geoff Wragg in 1992, who won it in 4.54.15, and quicker than Stratum in 2022, a nine-year-old ridden by William Buick and trained by Willie Mullins who took the prize in 4.54.69 and a way faster than Overdrive, a four-year-old ridden by Steve Cauthen, trained by Henry Cecil in 1988 who passed the post in 5.01.91.

If something is worth having, it's worth waiting for. 'It was the single greatest moment as an owner in my racing career, my best day on a racecourse, and he's still the oldest horse in history to win the Queen Alexandra at Royal Ascot,' Piers says. 'The oldest horse before that was Brown Jack in 1934, aged ten.' Most special of all was that whenever he was in the winner's enclosure, Piers would go to stroke the horse and 'he'd always give me a huge nudge with his nose. Wonderful! As if to say, "I told you I could do it."' Patience well and truly rewarded.

* * *

Brown Jack won the race six times in a row, and like Caracciola, rejected convention and switched to the flat from hurdling. He won the Champion Hurdle at Cheltenham and had such a spectacular turn of foot his Irish trainer, Aubrey Hastings, asked the leading flat jockey of the day, Steve Donoghue, ten times champion jockey, six Epsom Derby wins, among others, if he thought Brown Jack would make a flat horse. Steve said yes, and not only that, he would ride him. Brown Jack's final Queen Alexandra win was his last ever race, and he gave a storming front-running performance (because the pacemaker failed to do his job), Steve had dropped his whip and they were in danger of being seen off by the four-year-old Solatium. When they won, grown men wept, and his trainer (by then Ivor Anthony after the death of Aubrey) couldn't bear to watch and sat alone in the paddock until he heard the cheers and knew. The horse lapped up the attention, and allegedly refused to enter the parade ring until the crowds had rushed back from the rails to cheer him in.

* * *

Looking back on Caracciola's career, Andrew Tinkler says now, 'To stay sound and sane at that level for so many years, with the constitution to race all year round, to be so good in all three disciplines, to be so tough, shows how good a mind he had. It's 100 per cent testament to the horse and to Nicky's magnificent training.' He remembers how easy the horse always was, and how clever. 'He was ultra professional in anything he did, a quick learner. Once a horse has an efficient hurdling technique, not many can adapt to jumping a fence and be as successful. He had a very good brain and mind; to take the training and the amount of racing, and be successful for so long at that level, and then successful on the flat during a jumping career is quite something.'

Caracciola was always looked after by Sarah Shreeve. She says, 'There was never a quiet moment! Even at 13, he wouldn't lead the string, a baby would have to lead him. He'd still whip around the whole time, he never cantered on our round gallops, he'd whip around into the middle.' She remembers, 'When the ground was hard, they'd put the hurdles on the all-weather and it would take a good week before you could get through the wings with him, he'd duck out the side and spend more time in the field than up the all-weather. He had plenty of character. He'd go out in the field every day and if he didn't, he'd get so mad, kicking the door.' She loved him dearly and when Piers commissioned a portrait of 'the hero himself' ('it cost more than the horse!') she cried because he had been so perfectly captured.

When he finally retired, Eddie took him on and remembers him as 'a complete gent. He had loads of manners; when you said to move over, he'd move over, he'd bend his head down to put the bridle on, stand still when you're putting the saddle on, he had a fantastic temperament.' Eddie took him hunting, and even lent him to a young girl in the village who didn't have her own horse to go showjumping; a late, final spin over jumps. There was nothing he couldn't or wouldn't do.

His career was a truly extraordinary accomplishment, from both horse and trainer, as Mick says, 'They found his niche and it was lovely to see him go so well at that age. Nicky sees things that not everybody sees and it shows his management of these horses, to bring them back. If they're losing the taste, it only comes out on the racecourse, and credit to the horse, they've got to want to do it, and he wanted to. That was the great thing about him.' He adds, as a true horseman, 'Horses will tell you things, if you listen.'

6

BINOCULAR

The playful natural athlete and brilliant Champion hurdler

The first thing Nicky said when we started talking
about this book was 'it's going to be really hard
to narrow it down to 12', and since then, he has
effortlessly batted away all my timid negotiations to
do so. So, the three horses here are all united as one,
by carrying the JP McManus colours of green and
yellow hoops. Binocular leads the charge, passing the
silks to My Tent or Yours who in turn hands them
on to Buveur d'Air, their stellar careers seamlessly
ebbing and flowing. 'They all have one thing in
common,' Nicky says, 'which is their ability to jump a
hurdle at great speed.'

NICKY HAD a Remittance Man flashback when he saw Binocular. He was good-looking, but lean like a scarecrow and when he called JP to tell him about the horse, he said, 'I don't need any more ponies.' Nicky had to make a decision. He ummed and ahhed all the way home, 'There's something I like about him, but JP says he doesn't want any more ponies. But I could see something was there. He could move, the form was good, he'd run on the flat, he'd never jumped a hurdle, he was very athletic. Is he big enough? No, but we can make him big enough. I said yes and waited until he arrived back at Martinstown and when there were no screams of, "hell's bells what have you done", I assumed it was alright. And they did a brilliant job with him. JP's team are very, very good. So, when he pitched up back with me, instead of having a twig I got a round apple. And he was brilliant.' None of which he could have foreseen when he first clapped eyes on this scrawny pony. 'No. But he was an athlete. So, you had a chance.' That's the eye, seeing something that others miss, assessing potential.

As a four-year-old, Binocular took Mick Fitzgerald for two mighty Juvenile Novices' Hurdle spins and he remembers, 'When I rode him for the first time at Ascot, I dismounted and I said to Nicky, "This horse will win the Triumph."' What gave it away? 'When you ride good horses, they give you a feel. It's like driving a fast car – if you put two cars alongside each other you don't see much difference until you press the accelerator. He had a lot of natural pace, a good jumper, very fast over the obstacles, and when he won, I thought, this is a good horse.' They won that debut by six lengths and Mick says it wasn't just the win, 'it was the manner of how he quickened away, when I asked him to go, that I was so impressed with. When you pressed the button, it was a very quick response. It was an ordinary race, but it didn't matter, the feel the horse gave me was different. Over time you can just feel it, and he felt really smart that day.'

A month later, the winning duo headed to Kempton where they triumphed in the Adonis Novices' Hurdle, but Mick was disappointed and this time he told JP, 'I thought he was a better horse than that.' It later transpired the horse had a few physical issues which would stalk him through his career. Mick says, 'I was dismissive about the horse he beat, as I'd thought he was an aeroplane when I won at Ascot, and he made such hard work of it,' though he reconsidered when the horse he beat – Pierrot Lunaire – went on to win the Novices' Hurdle at Aintree and Binocular went on to greatness of his own, proving Mick right. As he says, 'I'm pleased that he went on and did what he did. Very often a horse gives you a feel and it's nice when that's borne out down the line.'

AP McCoy became his regular jockey (and JP McManus's retained jockey from 2004 until his retirement in 2015). When it came to the best way to ride this horse, AP was aware of the 'very respectful relationship' he had with owner and trainer: 'The two have a wealth of knowledge and thankfully have been around a lot longer than me, and seen a lot more than I have,' while also being AP enough to add, 'both know I like to do what suits me best, hopefully that works out alright. If the ship's going to sink it may as well be me taking all the blame.' He brings skills that, alas, can't be taught, as he explains, 'in sport, it's about making instinctive decisions better than anyone else and more successfully than anyone else,' so while the three of them could talk and talk, once he was out there, he was on his own, knowing that the strategy they had devised could suddenly be as outdated as a brick-sized car-phone and a new one must be invented, literally on the hoof. 'You go out with a plan, you think this is the plan, you've also got to be able to think this plan might not be the plan.' Bottom line, 'When the tapes went up, I knew I was OK at riding.'

Corky speaks truth to power and remembers an early exchange with AP about Binocular. 'He said, "This horse will never win a Champion Hurdle,"' Corky says. He takes comments like that personally; these are his horses. 'I said, "He will if you let go of his head," and he never spoke to me for three months after that.'

AP wouldn't forget an exchange like that. He responds, 'I did let his head go in the Supreme Novices' Hurdle and he got beat, that was the problem, so it was. He took it up at the last and he got beat by one of JP's other horses, Captain Cee Bee, which really pissed me off.' It may still bother him; time doesn't seem to have its usual power to soften the corners and bleach the colours for athletes when it comes to winning and losing, though AP happily admits, 'Corky knows his horses.' It was the only race of that year that the duo didn't win; they took home juvenile Novices' Hurdles at Ascot, Kempton and Aintree and then the Betfair Hurdle at Haydock and the Grade Two at Ascot.

Luckily his lad, Jake Loader, got on terrifically well, loved riding Binocular and always thought he'd have a nice career in dressage if the racing hadn't panned out. He remembers, 'If you trotted him at full speed, he'd really throw his toes out like a dressage horse going into the extended trot.' One day, the horse was being 'scoped', where a video endoscope is secured up the horse's nose, attached to a piece of kit on the bridle and links to a recorder and power pack in the saddle, to discover any breathing or wind problems, he says, 'I was doing a scope on him with all the mechanics and while I galloped him, Charlie Hills was driving alongside and he was like, "Oh my God, look at the movement, what is that?" When he was told who it was, he said, "I never would have guessed that horse would move like that, the way he was extending trotting, flipping his toes out."'

'He was a bit of a show off as well.' His usual way of going about his day was to buck all the way to the gallops (if Jake laughed, he'd drop his shoulder too), take a hold when he was there, and train himself. 'He was clever,' Jake says. 'You were just a passenger and he'd do what he wanted to do: right, done my bit of work, just going to cruise to the end of the gallop, not going to overdo it, I can't be bothered.' Corky would tell Jake, 'Don't just sit there on him, make sure he's doing some work.'

Nicky at home with Champ, Seven Barrows, August 2023.

Amateur jockey Nicky and Happy Warrior (r) upsides at the last, on their way to their first win, Kempton, 16 November 1972.

'His neck was getting longer and longer, the saddle had started to go backwards and I thought I was going to run out of rein.' Nicky and Happy Warrior (r) clear Becher's Brook on their way to victory despite serious tack problems in the Fox Hunters' Chase at Aintree, 1977. [George Selwyn]

0   b g Gallant Phoenix—dam's pedigree unknown
     Mr J. J. Kirkpatrick   Mr C. Kirkpatrick
                  (J. Kirkpatrick, Bourton-on-the-Water)
     AZURE BLUE, RED, WHITE and BLUE sash, BLACK
     cap   (Heythrop)

514 HAPPY WARRIOR .... 10 12 0 ......   *The 1977 Fox Hunters' Chase racecard.*

          Gr g Combat—Chunky Clemantine
111/2-P4 Mr N. J. Henderson   (F. T. Winter, Lambourn) Mr N. Henderson
          WHITE, DARK BLUE hooped sleeve

     515 HARRISON

Fred Winter in 1973; master horseman, four times Champion jockey, eight times Champion trainer, his methods still used by his protégés to this day. Nicky spent five years as his assistant, and says, 'The whole Winter family became like brothers and sisters, like my family, for a couple of years.'

Zongalero and Bob Davies chase the winners Rubstic and Maurice Barnes in Nicky's first attempt at the Grand National in 1979. Bob says, 'He was fantastic all through the race, he got leg weary after the second last.'

John Francome gets hung up on The Reject in the Arkle, Cheltenham Festival, 1985. John remembers, 'It was a fall you couldn't have done in 100 tries,' and he stood himself down for the day. Steve Smith-Eccles picked up his ride on See You Then. [George Selwyn]

Steve Smith-Eccles congratulates See You Then after their first Champion Hurdle win at the 1985 Cheltenham Festival with head lad Corky, Nicky and stable lad Glyn Foster. Steve remembers 'On the run in, I gave him a little nudge … and that was it. It was so easy.' [George Selwyn]

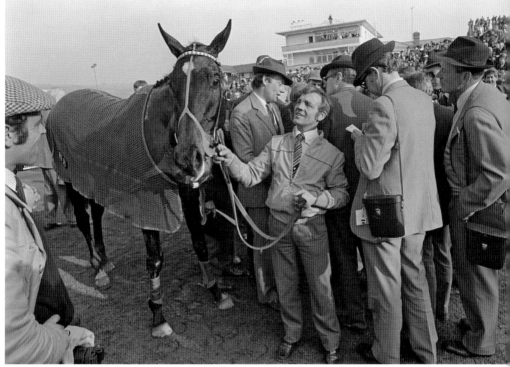

Nicky talks to the pressmen about his first Festival winner, Glyn only has eyes for See You Then. Glyn was the only person the horse would tolerate in his stable. For everyone else, Nicky says, 'You'd go into his box, he'd grab you, and while you were turning to get out of his way, he'd kick you!'. [George Selwyn]

See You Then, ridden by Steve Smith-Eccles, on the way to a second Champion Hurdle victory in 1986 and showcasing what Nicky describes as the horse's 'unique ability to cross hurdles at speed like an arrow'. [George Selwyn]

Remittance Man with his team; devoted lad Iain Major and constant companion Nobby the sheep, 1994.

Remittance Man and Richard Dunwoody flying to victory in the Hopeful Chase at Newbury, 1990. Richard says Nicky's instructions were generally no more specific than, 'You know what to do, kick on from the second last, try not to over-complicate, try to get the lead over the last.'

Jamie Osborne on
Remittance Man
(l) and Richard
Dunwoody on
Waterloo Boy (r)
in the 1992 Queen
Mother Champion
Chase.

Owner Tim Collins
(l) leads Jamie and
Remittance Man to
the winner's enclosure,
Richard Dunwoody
can be seen behind.
Richard remembers,
'It was particularly
galling when Jamie
came screaming past me
… that the way it goes,
I hope I congratulated
him … maybe.'

Jockey Mick Fitzgerald and Nicky after Caracciola's Maiden Hurdle win at Newbury, 2002. Mick says, 'I was always honest with him and he always made me think I was riding to the top of my ability. Having a trainer with that much confidence in you makes you not doubt yourself, and that's huge, because riding is all about confidence.'

Caracciola – with ears pricked – sets a record as the oldest horse to win at Royal Ascot when he takes the Queen Alexandra Stakes in 2009 aged 12. Jockey Eddie Ahern says, 'He loved the big occasion, he could feel the atmosphere of Royal Ascot, he'd come alive.'

AP McCoy and Binocular win the Champion Hurdle in 2010. AP says, 'I told Nicky, "If you didn't look straight ahead at the jump and you looked sideways, you wouldn't know if he'd taken off."'

Nicky has a word with Binocular in front of his Champion Hurdle trophy, 2010.

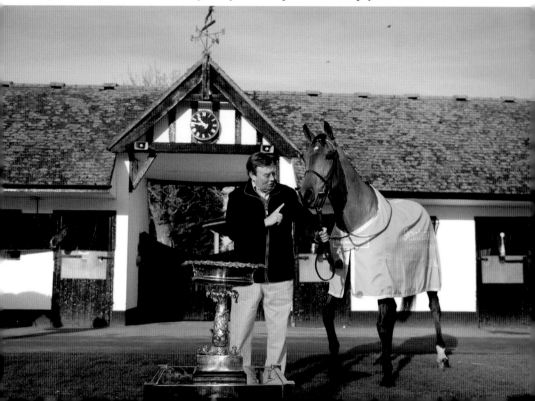

Nicky and stable lad Farhan congratulate My Tent Or Yours after winning the International Hurdle, Cheltenham, December 2017.

Buveur d'Air lands over the second last in the Grade One Fighting Fifth at Newcastle in 2019, with wood from the hurdle embedded in his foot. He finished a game second. Barry Geraghty says Buveur d'Air was 'the quickest I ever rode from one side of a hurdle to another'.

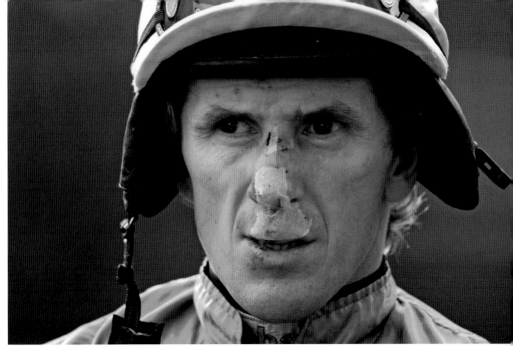

'I got kicked in the face at Wetherby, I had 25 stitches in my face and my front teeth were knocked out. I told the surgeon I needed to get stitched up immediately, and I got a dentist in Gloucester to make me new teeth at 11.30pm that night, because I wanted to ride this horse the following day at Ascot.' AP recalls his prep for his 2012 Novices' Hurdle win with My Tent Or Yours.

AP gets to his feet after a fall, Leopardstown Christmas Festival, 2014. 'I miss it,' he says, 'I miss the torture, I miss being miserable, I miss not being content, I miss the challenge, the chase, the routine, the structure, I miss winning, I miss the danger, I miss getting kicked around the place.'

The 2011 Cheltenham Gold Cup and the changing of the guard as Long Run (l) and amateur jockey Sam Waley-Cohen see off legendary chasers Denman and Kauto Star (r). 'It was the fantasy race,' Sam says.

Helen Stevens leads in Sam Waley-Cohen and Long Run. Sam was the first amateur to win the Gold Cup for 30 years.

Leaning in: Sam Waley-Cohen and Long Run (l) en route to winning the Grade One King George at Kempton, 2011.

At ease: Nicky with Long Run at Seven Barrows in 2013.

Barry Geraghty, lost in thought, after winning the 2013 Cheltenham Gold Cup with Bobs Worth, Cheltenham Festival 2013. Jockey JT McNamara had a catastrophic fall the day before and Barry remembers, 'All of our minds were on JT, he was a great friend of all ours, we were close over the years.'

Nicky congratulates Bob in the winner's enclosure. He says, 'There was nothing flashy, he would never have told you he was a Gold Cup winner at any stage of his life.'

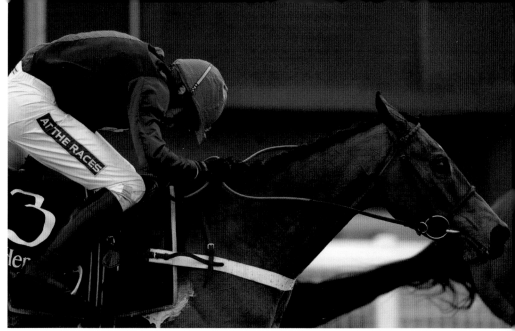

The ever gallant Bobs Worth and Barry Geraghty on their way to winning the Hennessy Gold Cup, Newbury, 2012.

A family of five: Bobs Worth in retirement with Tracy and Charlie, Harry and Oliver Vigors. [Debbie Burt]

Simonsig and Barry Geraghty take the 2012 Neptune Novices' Hurdle at a canter. 'We didn't know how good the horse was when we bought him,' his owner Ronnie Bartlett remembers. 'We had to pinch ourselves. Is this real?'

Simonsig with Triolo D'Alene, on holiday at the Vigorses' Hillwood Stud. 'They were brothers,' Nicky says. Tracy Vigors remembers, 'It was a proper love affair, I've never seen anything like it.'
[Tracy Vigors]

Jake left the yard before Binocular hit the big time. Recalling advice from Frank Conlon, former head lad to Sir Henry Cecil, now an instructor at the British Racing School, he says, 'He told us, "try your best not to get too attached; you love the horses, you'd do anything for them but they're not yours, the owner can take them away tomorrow, they could break a leg and you come home without them, so be hard in that sense,"' and Jake found he couldn't square it with himself; loving, but not too much. 'It's not fair on the horses,' he says, 'they are there to be loved and cared for, as I did, and they need that little bit extra.' It's a very noble exit. Horses can bring out a selflessness so willing, it might take some people by surprise.

AP remembers how Binocular flew: 'He was so quick through the air, it's hard to explain to someone who hasn't done it how much ground a horse can make at a jump from being quick. He made so much ground through the air, I said to Nicky, "If you didn't look straight ahead at the jump and you looked sideways, you wouldn't know if he'd taken off." He was that quick, all he'd do is lift his head and bend his knees, that's what makes a good hurdler, no other reason, and you can't teach it.' AP partnered him in 20 of his 22 hurdle races, and nine of his 11 wins.

But with his brilliance came back problems. Binocular wasn't so different from anyone when AP says, 'You got the best of him when he was feeling his best,' and 'it wasn't that he was soft, it wasn't a mental thing, it was physical.' It might sound simpler, to solve a physical problem than a mental one, but in a thoroughbred racehorse, there's no such thing as an easy fix for such logic-defying feats of engineering. Horses have 205 bones and around 700 muscles to keep in working order. He went off the boil in another trio of results, in the Festival's Champion Hurdle, the Fighting Fifth at Newcastle and the Christmas Hurdle at Kempton. The horse returned to Ireland for expert veterinary care then came back to Seven Barrows for the ministrations of one Mary Bromiley.

* * *

These days, Nicky has a physiotherapist on the yard every day and it's an almost traditional part of the five-star care package, and that's all thanks to the late Mary Bromiley MBE (Mary died in 2019). She was a true pioneer. Already a physiotherapist for humans, she came up with the idea for horses while stationed with her husband in Malaysia. She'd taken on injured racehorses, and was furious to discover all her brushes had gone missing, so she made her stable lads groom with their hands, which was basically massage, and the results were astounding. When she returned to England, she pursued it but it took years – decades – for people to take her seriously. Mary once visited Ron Smythe's yard in Epsom to look at a horse for him, came out of the box after five minutes and said that she couldn't find anything wrong. He said, 'Now I trust you, go and look at the one next door, that's the one with the problem.'

She bought a former racing yard just outside Lambourn and put in the first horse walker, outdoor arena, straight swimming pool and four sand boxes and her brilliant reputation grew.

Mary got Binocular right, with the help of Corky; she always said she couldn't work in a yard if the head lad wouldn't work with her. She discovered Binocular had a problem with the joint between his head and neck, and as horses use their heads to balance, if they can't balance, they can't use their stride, for galloping or jumping. She realised he couldn't use his head properly; she isolated the joint, treated it in a few minutes and then Corky went on and did what she had asked.

Mary had a deep love of horses too and once said, 'Horses are a different species and if you have the wit to try and learn about them, you will learn things that you will never learn from another human.'

* * *

Binocular's finest moment, the 2010 Champion Hurdle, nearly didn't happen due to a muscle problem, and AP was 'gutted that he wasn't going to get his chance; he got beat the year before, which was heartbreaking because I thought he should have won, and I was looking forward to going back that year, I thought he'd definitely win'. But miracles do happen and having been ruled out, Binocular was ruled right back in again. AP remembers the race as 'very straightforward, he was mid division most of the way, travelled, jumped really well and we came up by Celestial Halo two out. Down the hill he was cantering and when we came off the bend, he was always going to win.' His victory meant Nicky equalled Peter Easterby's record of five wins for the race (a record Nicky's since overtaken, currently standing at nine). He also returned to Kempton to take the Christmas Hurdle twice, before retiring at the end of 2013, due to a heart problem, and passing the colours on to My Tent.

Binocular returned to JP McManus's Martinstown Stud where he lives the life of Riley. Nicky says, 'JP loves his horses, he's the most incredible hoarder of old friends, he's got fields full of them – one has eight Champion Hurdlers.' Lara Hegarty runs that part of the yard, and sometimes doesn't answer her phone because she can't hear the ring tone *when she's vacuuming the barn*. She says Binocular 'loves his retirement, he's one of those horses in the field that's always in your face, trying to climb into the Jeep, he's always been very playful and cheeky. He used to go out with Istabraq but he was so giddy, galloping and messing, and Istabraq was following him and it wasn't fair on his legs to be that excited.'

* * *

My Tent took up Binocular's baton and was a rascal, as James Nixon who was charged with breaking him in can confirm. He was a contemporary of the impeccably well-mannered Bobs Worth, and My Tent decided to go another way.

Like anyone who's sat on a horse, James had been frequently un-sat but My Tent was next level. 'Back then he got me off quite often,' he remembers. 'Ben Pauling was helping me get on, and My Tent decided to fly me through the air, the first day we ever sat on him. He did that a fair few times.' Next time, 'he was sat on the lunge ring, and he was fine to start with, then all of a sudden, he realised I was on his back and decided it was a good idea to fly me through the air two or three times in one sitting. I called it a day as it was getting a little bit on the annoying side.' He was back for more, and Ben was delighted to tell James he looked like 'a starfish in the sky'. The next time he was more of a 'rag doll, he threw me so high I didn't know where the ground was, but it was nowhere near my feet,' and no horse left underneath him either. After that, it felt more like 'riding a bull in a rodeo', head down, back up, nowhere to go but up in the air. If he managed to stay in the saddle, his arms were flailing in mid-air like a one-man Mexican wave. 'I was a 17-year-old Jack the lad, thinking I could do it,' he says, 'and they were teaching me how it all worked by putting me on the most dangerous horse. When I fell off: get me back on again! Then he did it again. He was pretty naughty, but I got him going nicely and he turned into a good horse so we didn't mind.'

Once My Tent was broken in, his spirit was still strong. James remembers, 'He was a strange character. We'd go to the gallop and he'd decide it was a good idea to veer off the track, go and sit on the floor and try and roll over. Everybody else was in an orderly fashion and I was on the floor. Never had that before! He just decided it was a good idea. Luckily, I could jump back on; he'd do it in the stable too.'

It was all new to My Tent, and he handled it his way. He was young, 'finding out where his feet were, he was a bit stumbly as a baby, most are. He was strange, quite narrow, tall and lean, until he grew up a bit, filled out to be a really nice type, but he was leggy and all over the place.' James knows why he was so naughty: 'He couldn't quite physically do it, so he thought he'd mess around. You could feel he had something there; you didn't know whether he knew that. I never expected he'd have been as good as he was when breaking him in, he was a big silly baby who couldn't organise himself.'

Corky also had a soft spot for My Tent from the first day to the last and when My Tent retired, the farrier boosted Corky into the saddle for one last photo (he looks so entirely at home up there, you'd be forgiven for thinking, that looks easy, I must have a go).

JP McManus bought My Tent from his original owners, The Happy Campers. AP remembers, 'I won a bumper on him in Ludlow and I thought he was a very, very good horse, he had such a high cruising speed. He was second four times at Cheltenham and lots said maybe he didn't try as hard as he should, but he was very hard to settle. He needed a horse to go a suicidal pace in the first half of the race and he never got that, and we never saw the best of him. He'd have been much better, he used up so much energy in the first half of a race, he was so exuberant.'

The second places were 'heartbreaking' for AP (on this he's in total agreement with Corky who says 'the best place in the world is the Cheltenham enclosure, number one, there's nothing like it. The worst is number two'). AP missed his next two runs due to breaking his back and come his run in the Novices' Hurdle at Ascot, he had to put up with yet another poorly timed medical interruption. 'I got kicked in the face at Wetherby,' he says, 'I had 25 stitches in my face and my front teeth were knocked out. I told the surgeon I needed to get stitched up immediately, and I got a dentist in Gloucester to make me new teeth at 11.30pm that night, because I wanted to ride this horse on Saturday at Ascot.' The medics did as they were told, and he was back in time for the winner's enclosure.

When AP retired at the end of the 2014/15 season, Barry Geraghty partnered My Tent. He remembers discussing a hood for him because 'he was a strong puller and you're burning energy if you're pulling like that, running with the choke out'. He says he crossed a hurdle 'rapid quick', in close, a proper hurdler with scope, but using that scope through the race uses too much energy, so 'you find a rhythm and conserve, you're looking for an even rhythm, trying to meet that hurdle on a nice stride. It's as much down to the horse, he has massive ownership in this; it starts with schooling and works all the way through and there's no better yard in England and Ireland to school and prep a horse. It's Nicky's attention to detail, even schooling experienced horses mid-season, it's like muscle memory, the constant practice, training the mind as much as the body. The groundwork is unbelievable and they develop better technique for that and you can find that rhythm, slick and quick as you can, without burning too much so that when you need those big jumps over the last two or three, that's when you want them, keeping your powder dry.'

When My Tent was ready, having been second in the Supreme Novices' and three Champion Hurdles at the Festival, and winning the International Hurdle in his last Festival, as well as the Fighting Fifth at Newcastle and the Christmas Hurdle at Kempton, bringing his wins to seven, he handed the colours to Buveur D'Air. He followed Binocular to Martinstown where Lara says of this former rapscallion, he's now 'an old gentleman. He's so chilled and relaxed, we put him out with the youngsters, he keeps them calm. He's easy to catch so they're easy too, they won't go galloping, they graze, and copy him.'

* * *

Day one of Nicky's 'so-called week's holiday'. No phone calls, horses, problems, decisions. As if! Racing manager Noel Fehily called at breakfast to advise him that owner Jared Sullivan was selling all of his horses (he had seven or eight with Nicky) and 'they're all yours for three days, you can buy what you want, and here are the prices'. Number one on Nicky's list was Buveur d'Air.

'When we were doing the deal of buying Buveur d'Air, Noel Fehily was managing it and JP, off his own back, put in a clause that if for any reason Barry Geraghty couldn't ride him, Noel Fehily, who had ridden him the first year in all his races, would. And Noel said, "I think that will probably clinch the deal, don't you?" Fine. Done. And as it turned out, he won the Champion Hurdle on him. To be fair, for once I did get it right.'

Buveur was quick, slick, nimble and Nicky thought he 'ought to stay hurdling and he would win the Champion Hurdle' but he had two runs over fences instead and won both. 'So, you say, "What's wrong with that?"' Nicky says, 'Well for me, the problem was Altior was sitting up there, he was blatantly brilliant and Buveur d'Air was not going to beat Altior over fences. Buveur d'Air's technique over fences … he was hurdling them, he wasn't getting high enough, because he was such a good hurdler, because he was so flat and quick, he crossed a fence like you cross a hurdle. And that's not how to jump fences and sooner or later, one will trip him over. I didn't like his technique and you wouldn't change it, because that's the way he jumps. He wasn't a big flashy jumper, he was electric, quick flick, he was a hurdler and we knew hurdling was where he'd excel.'

Come December, Nicky and JP discussed the route. Nicky's argument was, 'Please will you switch this horse back to hurdles. He will win the Champion Hurdle. He won't beat Altior.' It was, he says now, 'a bit brave, because no one else thought he'd win the Champion Hurdle, except for me.' And, so they agreed. And he did as Nicky thought he would.

Buveur was to Nicky, 'a dear friend, lovely horse, very reliable. He probably never got the recognition he deserved; he had lots of success, he won two Champion Hurdles.' Barry remembers, 'He was the quickest I ever rode from one side of a hurdle to another, you wouldn't even know you left the ground – rapid, in close to it, like lightning, his shoulder would barely lift, he'd just bend his knees. When you're that good you're going to get it wrong on occasion,' like the time in his third Champion Hurdle, 'picking up half a stride early, he caught the top and was gone. His jumping was generally scarily slick, then he paid the price.'

Barry's best day with him was beating Melon in his second Champion Hurdle, by a neck. 'There was a bit of scrimmaging on the run down to two out,' he remembers, 'Ruby was in front and Paul Townend was sneaking through the inside, I was keeping Ruby in as much as possible and Paul was trying to get a better position on the inside; there was a bit of jockeymanship, all friendly rivalry, no words afterwards.'

* * *

Mick Fitzgerald says jockey racing chat is no more than the equivalent of flashing headlights at each other if someone's in the way. AP says he'd hear 'lads chatting' (sounds casual, don't they have anything else going on?), and he didn't take part, 'I'd got myself to worry about and I never gave it out after the race to lads who'd cut you up.' Instead, he'd file it. 'I was much more cynical, I'd say nothing but I'd spot an occasion later on, and I'd remember it, and think, I'll be in a position to make things a little bit more inconvenient for you, and it will affect you more than me.'

* * *

'We squared up in the straight, myself and Buveur and Paul and Melon,' Barry remembers, 'and I knew the longer I waited before I went for everything, the better, so I was hands and heels, hands and heels. We flicked the last as he would, lightning quick and I was hands and heels again for another 100 yards after the last, I knew if I could just stay at that, when I really needed him and I wanted everything, I knew he just had that little kick to beat Melon. I was saving my cards for the last 100 yards; he came up trumps.

'Paul was trying to come through on the inside and get ahead into a position and sit there and not commit,' he says, 'I needed him to commit or not go there at all, so keeping Ruby tight, applying a bit of pressure to stop him coming out to leave a gap for Paul, and me keeping pressure on his outside means Paul has to force his way in and he's committed or he doesn't commit at all. It's all black and white, no screaming or shouting, we're all three experienced pros, we knew what we were after, there were no words or any issue after, these are moments in a race in a Champion Hurdle. There are no freebies and no handouts.'

And that, Barry says, is 'instinct and knowing a horse well and knowing that type, knowing the feel you're getting back from the horse, is it time to go, waiting for the green light. You need to understand them to know when the green light comes on.'

* * *

Barry was practically born as the big-occasion jockey. He started in pony racing, and was champion jockey for the first time aged 20. He says now, 'I'm sure I was full of myself but I wasn't fazed by the pressure and the environment.' His early success came with trainer Jessie Harrington. He says, 'We always had a brilliant relationship and she trusted me,' so when things went wrong, such as when Barry fell off Moscow Flyer in the 2002 Tingle Creek (they won it the next year and the next) and again as favourite in the Champion Chase in 2004 (they won it the year before and the year after) she knew he wasn't to blame. 'She said, "silly old eejit", about the horse, never pointing the finger.' It meant he could do away with self-doubt and 'that's what cripples people on the big stage. You're riding on instinct and taking away all those pressures for me made it easier, likewise with Nicky and JP.'

* * *

At Newcastle for the Fighting Fifth, (a race he'd won the previous year by eight lengths, pushing the favourite Samcro and Jack Kennedy into second) the ever-valiant Buveur made a mistake jumping the second last and hit the top of the hurdle. A piece of wood went down his coronet band (where the hairline meets the hoof) and straight in, underneath the hoof. 'There's a picture of him landing, and there's this piece of wood sticking out, it's bare wood, sticking out the front of his foot,' Nicky says.

Buveur finished the race, and Barry remembers, 'I was gutted and rang Nicky and never for a second did he question what I did, it was all about the horse. He's brilliant and entertaining in interviews, but also kind and caring and that's not always the case in real life.'

Lesley Barwise-Munro is the senior veterinary surgeon for Newcastle Racecourse and remembers, 'He'd have been full of adrenaline, and he didn't pull up, he kept going as a brave horse. He crossed the finish line and as he came off track there was blood pouring out of the foot.' She's never seen an injury like it, 'not to that extent and certainly not on the racetrack. We've never had any splinter injuries at all and it highlights the vulnerability of using wooden fences.' She remembers, 'He came in acutely lame, and was taken across to the vet treatment area, and immediately the photographer John Grossick came across with a photo of the splinter in the horse's foot.' Part of the wood shown in the picture had come out, and without that evidence, the team would have been in the dark about the extent of it. There were 'obvious bits of wood coming out of the top of the band, we probed, then it all fell together and the photo guided us as to what had happened'.

Lesley spoke to her colleagues and got on with immediate treatment. They pulled out three pieces of wood that had gone straight down vertically behind the coronet band. Having seen what was removed, they wondered what else was in there, but it was very close to the coffin joint (inside the hoof), and Lesley said, 'Look, I think this will need surgery, I think we stop retrieving in case of any more damage. We had to think on our feet. A couple of us discussed it and we knew he'd have to go to surgery to check out that joint so we thought, we've just got to stop, quit while we're just ahead. That was the big, crucial decision, stop and let him go to theatre, there were pieces of wood deeper than we could feel and within reach of instruments.' The wound was flushed out, and Buveur travelled to the Donnington Grove vets with all the necessary medication including pain relief, and a foot cast (lightweight, easy to mould, hardens quickly).

He had a good year off, and returned for a second at Haydock and two more starts but his accident at Newcastle did for him. Nicky says, 'That was the end. We got him back into training, but

he was never sound again. They had to take the whole of the front
of his hoof off, they took thousands of pieces of wood out of his
foot.' Buveur d'Air went into honourable retirement, having clocked
up 13 wins over hurdles and two over fences, and earnings over £1.2
million, returned with love and gratitude to Martinstown, where
Lara says, 'He's very quiet to handle, he's grand, very chilled out.
He gets a bit quirky if he doesn't know you, you won't catch him
in the field, but he's very sweet. When he arrived, there was a big
photo shoot with all the Champion Hurdlers. They were all getting
giddy, wouldn't stand still, pulling us and you could have let him
go, he just stood there, quiet and gentle.'

* * *

The horses have taken to retirement well. AP called it a day having
ridden 4,348 winners and been champion jockey a record-setting
20 times in a row, every year that he was a professional, and he *still*
wished he had a ride in this year's Grand National.

AP broke all the records, and all the bones, by taking what he
calls a calculated risk. The bones he broke included cheekbones,
forearm, arm, wrist, thumb, leg, collarbone, (which he also
dislocated, but still did press-ups for the on-course doctor to prove
he was fit enough to ride the next race, and which was then broken
in a fall three days later) ribs, (and punctured lung, twice) both
shoulder blades, middle and lower vertebrae, fractured sternum,
tibia and fibula and a cracked eye socket. That's not counting the
broken fingers, nose and teeth, a dislocated thumb, stitches and
the concussions. 'I knew I was going to be, hopefully, everywhere
more than everyone else and that included being in an ambulance,'
he says. 'If I was going in more races, I'm hoping I'm taking more
risks, hoping I'm going faster than everyone else, therefore getting
injured more than anyone else and being in an ambulance more

than everyone else. You can't have one without the other.' It's a quid pro quo not many have had to or could accept, and he's the first to say that hardly anyone can understand how he feels.

All this for a winning feeling that he says – give or take a Gold Cup, his first on Mr Mulligan and his second on the much loved Synchronised 15 years later, and a Grand National on Don't Push It – vanished as soon as he was back in the weighing room taking the silks off. As he remarks, 'Everyone wants to know who's going to win the next race.

'As a jockey you're in a losing sport,' he says, 'you lose more than you win, and I will lose more than anyone else, [but] as long as I win more than anyone else, I'll be alright. I'd go to bed every night really insecure that I might not be any good tomorrow and when I woke up, I always thought: today is the day. Yesterday could have been horrific, beaten on five favourites, three fallers, but as I got older, I thought, no one cares about yesterday, it's history. Make sure today is the day.'

AP knows himself and he says soulfully, 'I miss it, I miss the torture, I miss being miserable, I miss not being content, I miss the challenge, the chase, the routine, the structure, I miss winning. In some ways, people think it's nuts, and it's hard to say it because I see life-changing and fatal injuries, but I miss the danger. Most jump jockeys say "oh, he's just trying to be a hero", but I do miss getting kicked around the place, I miss falling in a 20-runner race, thinking for 20 seconds, am I going to live or die, and when they've galloped all over you, you think, I'm still alive. It's an amazing feeling.'

It's not the best one, though. 'I miss winning more than anything,' he says. 'Really good sports people are egotistical pricks and genuinely believe everyone goes to watch them and no one else.' This is the big-race jockey par excellence talking when he says, 'It's the difference between people who are worried about something going wrong on the big stage and the people thinking they're only here to watch me, when you see 70,000 and you think, how lucky am I, getting to perform in front of all this lot.'

* * *

When Barry fell at Aintree in 2019, he broke his tibia and fibula (possibly from being kicked by the horse that ran over the top of him) and like most jockeys his first thought was what a massive annoyance it was that he'd have to miss the Grand National the next day. He remembers, 'I broke my leg, I was in absolute bits, my wife was due to fly in that night and the first person in was Sophie [Nicky's wife]. She babysat me. That's the team they are.'

While he was coming back from that injury, he never considered retiring. Once he was back in the swing, he 'started to reflect on what my future is. We all talk about getting out in one piece,' and his old friend JT McNamara's career-ending fall was a stark warning. He discussed it with his wife, Paula, before Jessie, Nicky or JP McManus, and came to a decision. 'I didn't feel I had anything more to achieve, and I didn't want to regret keeping going, as much as I was still loving it. No regrets.'

7

LONG RUN

The imperious and thrilling Gold Cup winner

ONE SUMMER, the family Waley-Cohen, Nicky and Minty spent a sweltering May Day at the racetrack, Auteuil, in the Bois de Boulogne outside Paris. It was 2008, and it was exactly the kind of adventure that Robert wanted when he started owning racehorses, rather than riding. He's steeped in horses, takes pleasure in all the different aspects of racing – even the disappointments – and he wanted to be involved. This ruled out the Fred Winters of the world for him because he says with self-deprecation, 'They were the same age as my father, it would be a different relationship. They're more knowledgeable than you'll ever be and they're not interested in your ignorant and juvenile thoughts on life.' Nicky, however, is. He's a social animal, his phone rings constantly and he always answers it, he has a genuine gift for friendship. As Robert says, 'He makes great relationships, he's good with people in every walk of life, he makes it fun.'

The three-year-old Long Run caught Robert's eye immediately as a son of Libertina and half-brother to Liberthine, who he had owned as a racer when she gave Sam his first Cheltenham win in 2005. Long Run was already familiar with the racetrack. Nicky explains, 'The French race at three, four and five years old, and then game over, they've done so much so young, and we haven't started. We race at six to ten and we think they are their best years.' A three-year-old horse is roughly equivalent to a teenager, with five being early 20s, and the years of six to ten are mid-20s to mid-30s.

Robert remembers falling for Long Run immediately. The horse was 'perfect, exactly what a horse ought to look like, he had presence, athleticism and class'. All of that, and there was that family connection, though Robert is relaxed about the importance of breeding, saying, 'It's really nice if it happens, it isn't central. Before they run it's essential, after they run, you're buying on form.'

Long Run won, Robert got carried away and announced, 'Let's buy the bloody thing! Wonderful!' Minty was despatched to come back with a price. He did and it was huge. 'It was an outrageous sum of money,' Robert remembers, 'I said to my wife, "Christ! that's a lot of money."' She encouraged him, and Long Run was his for six figures ('definitely not seven'), which was far more than he'd ever paid for a horse.

Long Run completed his four-year-old career in France, beating Blue Bresil on his debut. Blue is now a champion stallion, and the sire of a horse called Constitution Hill. Long Run was the opposite of a rough diamond when he arrived at Seven Barrows, he was polished and accomplished with a big reputation. Nicky describes the horse as a 'very shrewd purchase' and adds, 'Long Run was talented but he'd done a lot before he got to us, he'd won a couple of Grade Ones in France, so he was already half way through his career.' His ways were ingrained, his style was set.

The Long Run experience was always going to be a family affair. Nicky and Robert have been close forever; Robert has had horses with him for the same amount of time. It's all been 'tremendous fun, we've never disagreed, he's wise, understands breeding and loves planning', Nicky says. Robert explained from the very start that his son Sam would be riding this horse. He remembers, 'Nicky was superb about it and said, "that's great, Sam rides him, that's straightforward, very simple". People said to Nicky once or twice, "Wouldn't he do a lot better with another jockey?" and Nicky always said, "He might but Robert's bought him for Sam to ride, so that's the deal."' Sam was then a young and talented jockey, still a claiming amateur (given a weight allowance in races), a bit like a provisional driver, and there were plenty of noises off. Sam says, 'I was deaf to the commentary, because you expect it, and in the end, Dad and I were doing it to have fun and enjoy it. It was noise, it was just white noise. People are going to have an opinion. That's fine.'

If the horse felt overwhelmed by his new quarters, he didn't show it. Helen Green (now Stevens) worked for Nicky for some years and remembers Tom Symonds riding 'Lennie' (his stable name). 'The shapes he used to throw!' she says. 'Tom used to just laugh, he rode with a loose rein, when he was throwing shapes, he didn't move, he had the best balance, he didn't flinch, I was in awe of him.' A few years down the line when it was Helen's turn, she'd plead with Lennie, 'please don't'. She was thinking, if I fall off, I'm in a lot of trouble, I'm on £1 million-worth of horse. 'I don't think I've ever felt anything as powerful as he felt.' She says now, of those times, 'It's a mad sport. In, say, tennis, you watch the people who compete at the top level, you don't play tennis with Federer. But we'd ride the gallops with AP and Barry, which was nerve-wracking but an amazing experience. There aren't many sports where you do that. Some of the boys who wanted to be jockeys were riding next to AP.'

For Sam, riding Long Run was like 'trying to contain a volcano. He was very, very boisterous, and still is, even to this day. He was a sort of boxer-meets-ballerina – huge power and athleticism – and you just tried to keep him contained and not doing any damage to you or himself. And just the most competitive horse in the world.'

There was no such thing as a companionable canter for this horse, he always played to win. Once when a group of journalists was crammed into Nicky's Land Rover to watch the gallops, they drove quite close to him. Lennie took up the challenge and accelerated strongly. The Land Rover did the same to keep up with him. Robert remembers, 'It was the only time I saw Sam get really angry with Nicky. He said "Get away! Stop chasing me, you're going to kill the horse! He's not going to be beaten by a Land Rover."' Sam recalls it all too well and says, 'He's a horse that wanted to have his head in front at all costs. And with great self-belief, so he would have definitely believed he could have beaten the Land Rover, and wouldn't have stopped until proven one way or another.'

There was worse to come for Sam. He says, 'We were schooling next to the best horses at Nicky's, riding with Barry and AP; guys really in their pomp. And I have to say, the whole string, circling, watching, is the most terrifying experience you could have in racing. You'd think lining up at the Gold Cup's scary, but it's nothing compared to schooling at Seven Barrows with everyone watching and opining and all the rest of it. And, he actually always scored well, though even when you'd done a strong piece of work with him, he bounced you all the way to the bottom, trying to go faster and exhausting you. Even at walk he would basically half-run off with you. Those schooling mornings matter. In the weeks before the Cheltenham Festival, they are quite intense.' It was an unnerving experience, like trying to defuse a grenade while the Royal Logistic Corps looks on, and Sam rose to the occasion.

AP remembers schooling Binocular for the last time before the Champion Hurdle and for that final pop, he would always 'go rather quickly' he says. Sam was on another of Robert's horses, Stravinksy Dance, and 'fair play to Sam he jumped out and went toe to toe with me ... it was the fastest he'd ever been over those hurdles'.

Helen was always proud of Sam, 'There's no one I'd rather watch round the Grand National, he's the most successful jockey over those fences, and once at Punchestown on Long Run, he dropped his whip landing over the second last and *caught it from behind him*. I remember being in the dope box afterwards – standard procedure – and all the vets and stewards said how amazing it was.'

If Sam battled nerves in front of his pro peers, Long Run didn't. He was a horse who felt supremely good about himself, including his cavalier jumping style. Nicky says it's common in French horses because in Auteuil they have 'big hedges that you jump through the top of. Ours are much stiffer, you jump over the top of them. We had to teach Long Run quite a lot, it wasn't easy for Sam either, he did really well. If the horse couldn't find the right stride, he'd bulldoze the fence.'

* * *

Long Run and Sam started big; their first race was the three-mile, Grade One, Novices' Chase at Kempton on Boxing Day. Robert remembers, 'When he walked into the paddock, he looked around as if to say, "Ah, so my subjects have come to admire me!" I mean, he looked like an emperor. He was a gorgeous, handsome, precocious, proud, confident horse. That's what it's all about. When you see something in its pomp, and knowing it's in its pomp.'

To put it another way, 'He was always a two-person lead-up,' Helen says. 'He was such a powerhouse, he'd push you into the railings. He was bouncing off the walls, and he was always saddled in the stable yard.' Once Sam was on board, she'd say, as she said every single time, she let a horse go, 'Good luck, stay safe.'

Sam's instructions were to get a good lead, but as he describes the (lack of) control he felt he had, he may as well have been instructed to give it his best dressage pirouette. It was a magnificent race, he remembers it with great modesty. 'He basically ran off with me, for the entire course, which was terrifying. If you actually rode him into the fence, vigorously, he absolutely pinged past everybody else, and all I could do then was haul him back and get behind the others again, and if I didn't boot him into the fence, he didn't bother to jump it very high. He just thought I'm a big strong boy, I'll just boof it out the way. He was a nightmare ride. Anyway, I remember seeing Ruby, coming round the final bend, and nothing in front of them, Ruby said "my horse is empty, you'd better go on now".' That classic jockey ruse again; was he working out how to get Sam beaten or did he really have nothing left in the tank? Sam decided to 'stop clinging on for dear life – my arms had given up – and he took off like a rocket and won by mile. I was trying to, more or less, keep a lid on things without doing anything too crazy. One of the big things was using his athleticism, not trying to suppress it, so to go long at fences, because he showed them so little respect, if he ended up shorter then he'd tend to crash through them. And he was still absolutely buzzing at the end.' It was spectacular; an amateur, a four-year-old and a 13-length victory.

After this Robert had what he describes as a debate with Nicky (the very reason that he signed up with him), about where they should go next. Nicky won that round (resulting in a first place in the Kingmaker Novices' Chase at Warwick) and by and by the horse arrived at Kempton for the King George, the three-mile Grade One Chase which he tornadoed through to win by 12 lengths from his stablemate Riverside Theatre, 'which is a long way in a Grade One!' Robert says, 'That was pretty special.' Long Run was taking the Waley-Cohens on the ride of their lives.

Nicky doesn't go in for detailed race instructions, or recriminations afterwards. When Sam fell off, he remembers getting a raised eyebrow but no more. 'Generally, he was incredibly sporting,' Sam says, 'Particularly on Long Run, because there's so much pressure. The days when you didn't win – assuming you hadn't made a mess of it – he was the first to come up to you and say, "Look, we did everything we could, don't blame yourself." I think he half saw part of his job to give me the confidence as well, in order to ride him well.'

It never occurred to Long Run to take it easy. As time went on, he would warm up by himself, and avoid the schooling ring for cantering left and right because he couldn't do it without taking everyone on. He was full on, regardless of the circumstances, like someone bowling bodyline balls at the village cricket match. Sam came to know the horse's confidence well. 'In the big races, the margins for who does or doesn't win are so fine that you really need to understand what you can ask, and when, and what's not going well,' he says. 'In races like the Gold Cup you have to be prepared to ask some fairly outrageous questions of your horse. And if you know them well, you know whether they're likely to give you the answer you're looking for. Knowing his desire to win and his athleticism could give me the confidence to ride him, and ask the questions that you end up asking.'

His path was mapped. Nicky works back from the Festival, not forward to it. He had the Gold Cup in his sights for this horse. Helen says, 'I don't envy Nicky; so much time and effort goes into one race; from the moment the horses are back from their summer break, the whole training performance for this day is quite nerve-wracking.' Some days leading up to it, she was too scared to speak to him, other times, 'all he wants to know is if your horse is good'.

Long Run would be the first to tell you he was not good, he was great – and that he ran in three Gold Cups. A few weeks before his first tilt at it in 2011, Helen remembers, 'Tom rode him every day and he stopped eating – not Tom – and Tom would spend all night in his stable, and be first on the yard to make sure he'd eat something. It obviously didn't hinder him but Tom put his all into every horse and Long Run was pretty special to him. He never went off his food again.'

* * *

The reason he stopped eating could be pure coincidence, or possibly, he was picking up microscopic signals in the yard that something was afoot; a crackling tension in the air, processions of people trying to read his runes. Horses pay more attention than undercover officers scanning a crowd on a royal walkabout.

In an experiment set up to test if a horse can pick up on a rider's anxiety, a riding school group were told to walk up to a bollard and back three times, and warned that on the fourth time someone would open an umbrella. The riders and the horses all wore heart monitors. On the fourth go, no umbrella was opened, so there was no reason for the horses' heart rates to rise, and yet the heart rates for both the riders and their mounts rose significantly. Linda Keeling, Professor of Animal Welfare at the Swedish University of Agricultural Sciences led the study, and says the riders were prepping for their horses to react, in subtle, microscopic ways, such as minuscule changes to their breathing, or an almost indiscernible tighter grip on the reins that were invisible to the researchers, but were clocked by the horses.

'Horses are very sensitive to picking up subtle signals from humans,' she says. 'It's deeply ingrained behaviour for a prey species to be sensitive to any potential danger and the heart rate going up is a need to prepare for flight or fight, sending oxygen to muscles.' That said, the results were unequivocal. 'I was surprised that it was as clear as it was,' Linda says. 'We set the experiment up because we thought this was what would happen but I didn't expect it to be as synchronised as it was and when we were doing it, we weren't very optimistic. We didn't see any differences, we didn't see people tensing up and shortening reins, the majority were very good at hiding subtle changes in behaviour from us.' One of her conclusions from this study is that, 'Horses are much better at reading us than we are at reading them.'

* * *

Come the 'Golden' hour, Nicky says, it's the same sensation for every single horse that he sends off, from the good to the moderate. Part of him goes with them, and 'you always have that gut-wrenching feeling when they go down to the start, and what's about to happen, for a big race with a fancied horse or for another at Plumpton on a Monday night – that's that owner's Gold Cup-day. There are lots of days when you know you're probably not going to win, but I like to think most horses we send out have got a chance of winning. Disappointment is horrible, but you've got to get back out there, get your horses out tomorrow.' Perhaps that's the pay-off, the winning feeling doesn't last, but then neither does the dismay? 'That's probably true.'

Nicky had found circling at the start of a big race as a jockey a lonely place to be with the world watching on. Not for Sam at the Gold Cup start; he says, 'Do you know, I never thought about it as being lonely, because I always felt that the horse and I were the partnership, so we were in it together.' That feeling – we two are one – unites all riders.

'There's no question everyone else is the competition,' Sam continues, 'but I always felt a great sense of partnership with the horse and direction, in terms of what we were trying to do. So, I wouldn't say it was lonely. I remember being very focused. Once you get to the start, in a way that people probably don't recognise, the race has started. It's not when the flag drops. You're already very much in the race, getting the position, being with the horse that you want to be with, and the tactics start the second you arrive. I was always concentrating too hard to be anything other than in the moment. It's a sort of meditative sport, because your field of vision is so narrow when you're on a horse.'

Robert recalls AP McCoy saying the Gold Cup is the toughest race because it's full on from flag fall, the best horses, the best jockeys, the best race and AP says now, 'It's end-to-end, no let-up, you don't win the Gold Cup and not be at the peak of your health, at the absolute top.' The 2011 Gold Cup was a who's who of spectacular chasers, names such as Denman ridden by Sam Thomas, Kauto Star with Ruby Walsh, Neptune Collonges and Robert Thornton, Imperial Commander and Paddy Brennan.

Robert remembers watching Denman and Kauto Star going 'hammer and tongs all the way down the hill and Long Run was just hanging on to their coattails. He didn't jump brilliantly round there. He made some mistakes. Sam rode him with great skill. And then he got to the bottom of the hill, with the two in front, and he sort of got a second breath. He couldn't come down the hill as fast as those two did in front of him, but on rising ground, he absolutely could. I can't tell you the excitement as he jumped upsides at the second last, and then went on at the last. It was unbelievable.'

Remembering now a conversation he had with Nicky who'd said, 'You know, most of owning racehorses is expense and disappointment, and things don't go right, so why do you do it?', Robert had replied, 'Well, you could talk to people who've done everything, been everywhere, are rich enough to have any experience in the world that you can possibly imagine – when did they last jump up and down and shout their heads off for two or three minutes? And the answer is, for all of them, never. So that's why I do it.'

For Sam, it was 'the fantasy race. He was a handful. He pinged the first couple, then he got too keen and so I had to start asking long questions, and he gave me some and he didn't give me some. And then they really tried to turn the pace up after the water and to be honest, about three-quarters of the way into the race I thought, this hasn't gone quite as well as I'd have liked, I'm not quite sure this is going to finish as well as I'd like.

'But then, from the open ditch going up the hill, he absolutely pinged and he just kept finding a position, and as we came down the hill, I knew we were close enough, but I remember Denman and then Imperial Commander coming round the outside, thinking, right, we're in this now, this is war! Here comes the fight! And you do ask a lot of your horse, I mean probably for a mile of the race you're asking for everything they've got.

'But then there was a moment when he was just in enough of a pocket that there was nowhere for him to go. And so, it gave him half a chance just to take the pressure off. I knew he was so competitive, if he saw any clear air he'd go into it, so I was trying to keep him covered, jump the fences in position, and then hope when you saw clean air and could ask for the push, he'd give it to you.

'I remember coming round the corner, thinking, we're close, we're close, we're all out, but we're close enough, and he met the last two fences on the stride. You could ride those fences a thousand times and not meet them on strides where you can put the maximum length and pace over a fence, and it was all-out. It was stretching every sinew, and then landing after the last, thinking, we've landed in front! Just roaring up the last furlong-and-a-half, shouting at him with all my might, keeping him going forward, making sure he knew the competition wasn't finished until he was over the finish line.'

Long Run pushed Denman into a seven-lengths second; it was a changing of the guard and Sam says, 'In a way you raise each other up in these big races. The horse and the jockey need to become one to become more, and I think there's something special when that comes together.' As they circled on the turf, Sam remembers a brief moment of calmness: 'It's probably only ten seconds, where the noise of the crowd dissipates for a second because the race is won, and the noise of the wind in your ears and the noise of the moment just goes quiet. And then you have this very short window, before anyone gets to you, and you realise where you are, and what you've done. You suddenly understand the range of outcomes of that day. It might have been disaster. And so, all that emotion of what might have been comes pouring out of you. So, it's sort of exhilaration and relief at the same time. And then just a sense of jointness.' Is that intimacy? 'I think it is intimate – that's probably the right word – you know you have this bond that's formed in that second, you're the only two creatures in the world at that second that have done that thing, that are together.'

Helen remembers exactly how she felt that day, leading up Nicky's first Gold Cup winner. 'At first it was just pure elation for Tom, for Sam, for the Waley-Cohens and Nicky, and also relief. There's always a lot of speculation going into the big races. People like to downplay your horse and say he's not good enough but after he won, I just felt so proud of him for showing everyone how good he was. I also had high-school friends congratulate me who had no interest in racing, yet even they watch the Gold Cup, so you suddenly get an idea of the enormity of what Long Run had just achieved.'

* * *

If riding Long Run felt like sitting on an unexploded bomb, Helen saw another side of him. She says, 'I think he was claustrophobic; he didn't like noise, he always wore ear plugs at the races and on open days, he didn't like people crowding his stable. I spent most of the open day after he won the Gold Cup in the paddock with him, away, grazing him, and he was a lot happier for people to look from a distance. He didn't like the indoor school, he warmed up on the outside, he didn't like being surrounded. I often used to travel in the lorry with him, and there were certain partitions he preferred. You have to know them well, they're all so different and they soon let you know what they don't like. If he wanted fuss or affection, you could give it, but if he didn't want it, he'd let you know. He'd be a bit of a grumpy old man, he used to like fuss on his own terms. He knew himself quite well.'

After the Gold Cup, he won the Denman Chase at Newbury and another King George – no small feat but he was ever so slightly on the wane and when such bright lights are dimmed, it's a stark change. Helen says, 'I don't think he lost his personality spark, when I was there, he never ran a bad race, but the Gold Cup was so tough, it may have taken it out of him, and afterwards, all the publicity, getting paraded, being the centre of attention, maybe the whole package takes it out of them.'

His second King George was full of blunders and missteps but he still managed somehow to see off Captain Chris (Richard

Johnson), Cue Card and Joe Tizzard, Riverside Theatre and Barry Geraghty and The Giant Bolster and AP McCoy. Sam says, 'There was probably no race where he triumphed which was absolutely smooth. The Gold Cups where he didn't win were actually much smoother. Maybe he needed that boisterousness to put the fire in him for the biggest days. That second King George was really tough the whole way, and you were asking for things that you shouldn't have been asking for. So that was a great day.'

And all this from an amateur jockey, who was the first to win two King Georges, a Gold Cup, a Grand National and so on. It was family fun, times a million. Robert's as proud as punch: 'If you have someone who's enormously talented, it adds immeasurably to the pleasure. And I enjoyed a lot driving to the races with Sam, and walking the courses with him, and having a good chat about this, that and the other. It's good fun, chatting about life in general, and everything in between.'

The connection with this horse went very deep. When Long Run stalked into the parade ring in Auteuil, the Waley-Cohens recognised him, perhaps there was even a kinship, as a half-brother to Robert's Liberthine. Sam's first spin on her was winning a Beginners' Chase at Stratford in March 2004. That year was a devastating one for the family. Thomas, Sam's brother died in the July after enduring ten years of bone cancer. When Sam went on and won the Mildmay of Flete Handicap Chase at the 2005 Festival with Liberthine, it was 'a fabulous event', Robert says, 'the first good thing that happened to us after Thomas' death. It was a very, very bonding moment.'

Sam describes it as 'the lifting of a grey veil, a sense that life won't always be terrible, that you can go on, with your grief, and feel happiness again. When you have such pain, you go into your own world to think about how to recover from that, and you do need something that sparks you back, and is the catalyst.' It was unexpected, too, 'an outsider in a professional race? Impossible. So, it did feel like a fairy tale. Actually, more than any other race, that was the ultimate for us. It brought us all back together. It was a symbol of renewal.'

Horses are agents of change; their effect never fails. Robert says, 'They teach you tonnes about life; with horses there are lots of disappointments and lots of challenges, and you have to nurture them and care for them, and bring them along quietly, and teach them, and things sometimes go well and sometimes they don't.'

Nicky's first answer to what horses teach us about life: have fun. It's probably no more detailed than that because it's like asking him, 'do you like oxygen?' His second thought is 'you've got to live with the good days and the bad days, and there are more bad than good, so you've got to appreciate the good days'. His wife Sophie says, 'Trust: they have to trust you and you have to trust them.' 'That's true,' Nicky agrees, adding, 'you're trying to be a fitness trainer and a psychiatrist at the same time, their heads are very important. They're all different, it's like having a huge class of children and on any one day, if you have three-quarters of them in workable shape you're doing quite well.'

* * *

Long Run retired and Helen left Seven Barrows. She looks back on it now and says, 'How fortunate I was with those horses; it was a very special time and I loved it. The horses and the people. Corky had a way with horses, he could look over a door and before even touching a leg he'd see it. Every day he looked at every single leg, he knew every horse inside out.' Nicky was 'so knowledgeable, old school, very jovial, he wanted everyone to have a nice time and work hard and get on as a team. He'd know if you didn't do your horses properly, and you'd know that he knew.'

He was also 'brutally honest; if you fell off, he'd say, "What on earth did you do that for?"' She remembers a horse, in training at the same time as Long Run, called Sentry Duty. 'Before a run at Cheltenham they'd make him really fresh, so he was buzzing. One day I rode him, I was petrified,' she says, but the gallops had been and gone and all was well. They were on the way home, walking along the lane, in a pair, when a postman arrived. Helen stepped Sentry onto the grass, he erupted, she fell off, he charged into the yard, stirrups flying. This chain of events takes milliseconds. She heard, 'WHO FELL OFF SENTRY?' 'I did,' she squeaked. 'WHO CAUGHT SENTRY?' 'I did,' she peeped. 'Oh, well done, are you OK?'

* * *

Long Run remains staggeringly competitive, though when Sam takes his daughter out for a ride on the leading rein, he's perfect. 'I think horses know when they've got to behave,' Robert says, 'he's incredibly dopey, leading them home, an old dobbin.' But when he's not setting an example to the kids, he prances, he's impatient, he's still got it.

Sam agrees, 'When he's in the yard he's pretty well-behaved, but even when you go out riding on the farm, he still tries to take on the ponies, and he stands at the gate and kicks out because he wants to get on with it. So, he's not a child's ride, I think it's fair to say. He's much-loved, but ride him with caution.'

Sam says looking back on these days that Long Run raised him up to a place he never dreamed he'd be, he was more than worthy of the partnership, with the two making something together that was more than the sum of their parts. But even more than that, he says, 'As a family it was actually more about the thrill of the day, as much as anything. Because we had wonderful days when it all went right, but actually the days when it didn't go right were also retrospectively good days. We spent the day together, with our hopes and dreams. So, it linked everybody together with an excitement and a joint purpose.'

8

BOBS WORTH

The unassuming and tough winner at three consecutive Festivals

THERE IS a distinctive, refined look about a Nicky Henderson and David Minton horse. Racing TV presenter Alice Plunkett says they are immediately recognisable on the racecourse, because, 'Nicky has a way of getting them fit when they don't look trained. If you walked into a paddock, you'd know his horses straight away, he gets them fit without them knowing it.' Nicky says they 'tend to buy elegance', horses that might make two-mile champion chasers and hurdlers.

Minty elaborates, 'They've got to have great presence, walk with a bit of a bounce, have an air of: "I'm great, look at me".' In a nutshell, 'the look of eagles'. It's a line from a 1937 poem written about Man o'War, the American racehorse considered so special – he won all 21 of his starts, established seven track records and raced at odds as short as 1/100 – that when he died, aged 30, in 1947 he was embalmed, lay in state in an oak casket lined with his colours, and his funeral with nine eulogies was broadcast on national radio. His devoted groom Will Harbut predeceased him, by a matter of weeks, and his obituary listed his survivors as his wife, six sons, three daughters and Man o'War.

> He was marked with the god's own giving
> And winged in every part:

128

The look of eagles was in his eye
And Hastings' wrath in his heart

Bobs Worth didn't have that look. He had been bought by Barry Geraghty as a yearling and went unsold the first time of asking, so he was back again as a four-year-old. Minty recalls, 'Going round the sales, Barry was looking a little forlorn, nobody was looking at his horse. Nicky and I thought he was a bit small and scopeless and he didn't walk like a good horse.' Barry admits, 'He probably lacked a bit of size and a little bit of scope, but he was a nice individual with a good way about him, a good attitude and a really good pedigree. He had a lot of Bob Back in him, he was good physically. You'd know a Bob Back: a nice type, not imposing but quality.'

Lois Eadie bred Bob in Brookeborough, County Fermanagh and picked Bob Back because 'he gives them great staying power. And the mare Fashionista was sired by Kings Theatre, a very good stallion, so there was a lot of speed all the way down that line.' There was also a sweet temperament on both sides, as Lois says, 'Fashionista was so kind, and very pretty with a gorgeous head that she passed on to Bob.' As a tiny foal, he was no bother to look after, 'terribly friendly, I'd go to feed them every day and they'd come racing up. He always had that wonderful nature, which helped him later, you don't want them too highly strung. He wasn't a huge robust foal, he was lovely quality, which he retained throughout his life.'

Lois had a veterinary team she could call in the middle of the night, to say: the mare's foaling! Come quick! Bring sandwiches! She remembers, 'When we'd foaled, we'd sit on a high trough to give the mare time to get on her feet and the foal to struggle to get up and we'd chat. With each one, we'd said, as a joke, "I wonder, will this be a Gold Cup horse or a Grand National horse?"'

Bob wasn't very big at 15.2hh, and scraped 16 hands as a four-year-old and he wasn't having a good day at the sales. Nicky and Minty walked into the ring, saw the reserve price of £20,000, and the bids stuck at £18,000, and out of affection and respect for Barry, they placed the winning bid. Minty said, he was 'one for the melting pot', bought on spec as all horses are, their talent a mystery until they set foot on the turf.

Bob arrived at Seven Barrows and as owners came to the yard to see the new arrivals, Malcolm Kimmins, known in the world as Kimbo, remembers, 'Bob didn't immediately grab one's attention, but we later discovered he was all heart.' Caro Wells, one of the five in their syndicate, the Not Afraid Partnership, took an instant shine to him which encouraged John Jarvis, David Nash and Nick Deacon on and they said 'yes'. Kimbo came up with the name, 'All simple stuff! Inexpensive purchase, now worth a bob or two. Also quite liked the rather doubtful connection with the famous fashion House of Worth for a Fashionista offspring but not sure anybody else did.'

'Kimbo has been a friend of mine for life,' says Nicky. 'It's not as though we can't disagree with each other, but we'll always get to the right answer somehow. We're very, very lucky. We have all the nice owners, we really do. I have the best owners out of any trainer in England. And things go wrong, and they get frustrated, yes, but they're the best of the best. And we're all good mates; and that's why we do it. I'm talking to them all day and night. They're lovely. It's their hobby and so we've got to make it fun.'

Alice Plunkett says, 'Nicky gets people in his team to invest themselves, and inspires such loyalty, people love being part of his gang. He's got a brilliant way of making things fun, and understands that he's got to entertain people, they're there to have fun, and also to deliver on the big day. It's an amazing mix.'

Bob was offloaded with low expectations, and, according to Minty, no particular skill in the purchase, but the right people met the right horse. They were very taken with him, and watched him working as often as they could. Nicky describes Kimbo as 'a very important person in Bob's life, he ran the syndicate, he made it such fun for everyone. If there are ten people, I can't talk to all ten all the time, so Kimbo passed info on. They've all got their opinions, it makes it all fun.' Kimbo agrees, he has great warmth and says, 'You walk through the front door, everybody's pleased to see you, you have an interesting, marvellous day because Nicky is a fantastic, kind host. It's a very happy place. I've been at it quite a long time from having horses with Fulke Walwyn – I'm the oldest of the gang – and it's a wonderful place to have a horse.'

Unassuming Bob may have been – if he could have tacked himself up, to save someone the trouble he would have done – but Kimbo is devoted and prefers to call it a 'lack of swank, he wasn't swanky'. Nicky says, 'If there were 100 horses, you would pick out Sprinter Sacre every time, you wouldn't pick out Bob. He had half of Sprinter's ability, he was a trier, not flashy – Sprinter was always, "I'm here!"' Nicky's partial to charisma, and he says, 'I can't say I was head over heels in love with him, he didn't have the glamour of a Might Bite, but he was an honest-to-goodness person, he wore his heart on his sleeve, he went out and fought for you. You couldn't have a more straightforward horse, you could set your clock by him, and he had the most fantastic temperament.'

Barry concedes he might not catch your eye on the gallops, but when he partnered him for his first bumper at Kempton in February 2010, 'he popped out of nowhere and ran a close second'. Kimbo remembers it well (it was his birthday) and, 'Nicky had a very good horse, Prince of Pirates, that was expected to win that day and he had our boy out for his first run, to take it easy, and suddenly to everyone's amazement, Bob was there and that's when Nicky realised there was a bit of talent there.' An unprepossessing character, but with a sprinkling of stardust too.

Nicky remembers, 'John Magnier – the son of Coolmore's JP Magnier – used to ride in bumpers for us, so he was going to ride, and we would introduce Bob to the racecourse. Being Bob, he hadn't shown us anything, but the other one had been catching pigeons and the whole of Lambourn knew about him.' Nicky gave Barry his instructions on Bob, saying, 'It's his first race, he's pretty one-paced, he's not a two-mile horse. You can make the running, you know where to go, where the best ground is, stay wide around that bend, down the middle, JP will follow you, you'll give him a lead. I expected six to have passed him.' However, Plan A is usually just a precursor to Plan B and sure enough, 'things go remarkably wrong, before going a furlong,' Nicky recalls. 'JP's horse tanked off with him, so he's in front, too keen. Bob sits behind him, with Barry shouting, "left a bit, right a bit", steering him round the course. Between the last two hurdles, which had been taken out, Barry suddenly cruises along on Bob and sits upsides JP. Luckily JP gave a nudge and a squeeze and beat Bob a length-and-a-half. After, I said, "JP, you gave me a fright! Why didn't you give him a smack?" and he said, "I didn't want to take my hands off the reins, I thought I might fall off." He was such a lovely guy, he was a star, it was great fun. They were great days.'

Bob had surprised everyone, and having been put away, he returned to begin his novice hurdling career, winning his first and starting an extraordinary run of winning six races on the trot, and beating well fancied horses like Rock on Ruby at Cheltenham, and Sire de Grugy by nine lengths at Kempton. 'He progressed and improved with every run,' Barry says, though 'he was a horse you had to protect, he wasn't as big and robust so you would nurse him through a race, and hang on to that trump card, save a little bit and then unleash him and he'd absolutely fly.' He was always so willing, as Nicky says, 'When you asked him the big questions on the big days, he was unstoppable. He'd put his head down and fight, not because he had raw ability – he didn't – but he was as tough as they come. What he lacked in ability he made up for in heart; he had the most incredible will to win, that's what won him all those races, he was so brave, he didn't know when to give up, he'd go beyond the call of duty.'

When Lois saw how valiant Bob was, and how successful, it was just the excuse that she and her husband had been waiting for to finally make the trip from Ireland to Cheltenham. She had seen his owners on television, so she knew what they looked like and, 'I went up to one as they came out of the collecting ring to go to the stands and I said, "You're one of Bobs Worth's owners, I'm the person that bred him."' They were surprised, and ran to see the race. He won, and back in the parade ring, they invited Lois to the podium. She said "Absolutely not." They said, "We don't go if you don't," and it's one of her most prized photographs, with his owner, and her hand on the trophy. From there, a friendship grew; every time Lois came to England, they'd all meet for lunch. 'It's unusual, you hardly ever get owners who are such wonderful people,' she says. 'People buy the horses, that's it, goodbye; they were different.'

Bob went on to surpass all expectations, winning three different races at three consecutive Cheltenham Festivals; the Albert Bartlett Novices' Hurdle in 2011, the RSA Chase in 2012 and the Gold Cup in 2013. This is a remarkable feat, not accomplished since the foul-tempered legend Flyingbolt in the 1960s. A week before the RSA, Nicky had a sleepless night, because he realised they were about to run Bob in the wrong race. Horses are never, but never, not on his mind. 'A silly thing came to me in the middle of the night,' he says. 'It occurred to me that Bob was not a two-and-a-half-miler, he was a three-miler. I was sure he'd stay, he loves that hill, we've got to switch.' He gave Kimbo the news first thing, and though he was taken aback, he happily agreed. 'I just know this is right,' Nicky told him, 'I just know.'

It was right, he did just know (though there's no 'just' about it), and when Bob won the RSA Chase in 2012, it was as part of Nicky's all-time great, record-breaking Festival. He racked up seven wins, including four on one day and five Grade Ones, which is about as easy as building a church in 24 hours. Sprinter Sacre won the Arkle by five lengths from Cue Card on the opening day. On day two, Simonsig won his first Grade One, the Neptune Novices' Hurdle, Bob took the RSA, Finian's Rainbow won the Champion Chase by just over a length from Sizing Europe, then 40/1 shot, Une Artiste, beat the boys to take the Fred Winter Juvenile Handicap Hurdle, Barry Geraghty gave Riverside Theatre a superlative ride to win the Ryanair Chase, and on the last day, Bellvano and Paul Carberry took the Johnny Henderson Grand Annual, named in honour of Nicky's father, who had formed a consortium to buy the course in 1963 and save it from closure.

At the photo shoot at Seven Barrows afterwards, to mark this extraordinary milestone, one of Bob's owners noticed Sprinter nodding at the audience, preening, while Bob 'made it quite clear he wanted to go back and have a quiet time in his stable'.

Bob and Cheltenham took to each other. Minty says, 'He'd pootle round in his own time, then storm up the hill,' and Nicky agrees: 'Bob would die for you. He'd potter along, fiddling away, you'd never notice him in the middle of a race, he wasn't showing off to everybody, but he has the biggest heart in the world, and he loved that hill at Cheltenham, his head would go lower and lower and if he got to the bottom of the hill and he was in contention, he'd win.'

Kimbo was so fond of Bob, he often couldn't face watching him racing. He was well known for disappearing on his own, as he says, to hide in the loos or 'behind the nearest bin' with eyes shut and someone giving him a rundown of what was going on. Come the 2013 Gold Cup, exceptional circumstances called for exceptional actions. Also, he couldn't find a bin. 'It was a wonderful day,' he remembers. 'There were 30 members of my family and friends around every corner, my children were there.' Kimbo's son failed to recognise his own sister because he couldn't see under her giant hat.

The Gold Cup is an unforgiving race, though Nicky says, there's a moment to fill your lungs 'if you get the moment right – and that's an art – if you're in an end-to-end gallop all the way, you've got to get a blow in somewhere'. Barry knows every inch of the Cheltenham turf and he knew Bob inside out. He recalls the ride: 'The whole way through, I knew the ground was a bit soft for us, he was struggling. I was nursing and nursing him all the way, trying to hang in there but trying to save that bit, and coming down the hill three out hanging in, I hadn't given up.'

Bob was nearly brought down by Silviniaco Conti falling at the third last. Barry manoeuvred past, but it meant they lost momentum and it made things more difficult. Lois remembers the grandstand giving an awful sigh and groan as Bob 'half swerved, half jumped over him and he lost about seven lengths. To lose seven lengths at Cheltenham especially the Gold Cup, you've no chance after that. Barry sat there and let him get his wind back and let him get going, and the rest is history.'

Barry continues: 'I wasn't as hopeful as you'd love to be [after the third-last] but as we turned into the straight and faced the second last and the two horses in front started to struggle a little bit, it was only then I asked Bob for maximum effort and the response was instant. As we faced the second last, it was a green light moment, all the lights went green.'

Kimbo remembers the commentator's words: 'This could be attritional up this hill, this muddy hill, this mercilessly muddy hill and here comes Bobs Worth!' It's one of the great cries, he says, 'here comes Bobs Worth'. He saw off Sir Des Champs and AP McCoy, Long Run and Sam Waley-Cohen, and The Giant Bolster and Tom Scudamore.

Lois says, 'It was unbelievable, I was shaking nearly all day,' and as she went into the grandstand, she 'happened to say' to the man on the gate that she had bred Bob. 'To watch your beloved horse that you've bred, taking off and running in the Gold Cup was absolute magic. And very nerve-wracking; I could hear my husband in one ear counting down as he got safely over a jump and I was watching through the binoculars. It's one of the greatest races, and only one horse, one jockey and one trainer can win, out of hundreds of horses trying to be good enough to run in the Gold Cup and as it unfolded, words couldn't describe it. When he won, we were jumping up and down and hugging and we went to the gate to go out, the man slammed the gate shut, gave me a big hug, lifted me off the ground, then opened the gate and said, "now you can go"!'

It was emotional for all connections: all three generations of Kimbo's family loved Bob. Jane, Kimbo's wife, remembers five of their grandchildren being allowed out of lessons to watch the race in the headmaster's study and another grandchild took a copy of the *Racing Post* with Bob on the cover and Kimbo on page 2 to her 'show and tell day' at her smart London school. For Lois, her foal had grown into the Gold Cup-winning horse that she and her vet always wondered about; Barry had just won the race of races on the now eight-year-old horse he always believed in and had known since a yearling, but his overriding feeling that day was for jockey JT McNamara who had had a catastrophic fall the day before. 'All of our minds were on JT, he was a great friend of all ours, we were close over the years. I'd love to have said it was a more joyous occasion but it wasn't as our minds were elsewhere. Reflecting back, it was a brilliant day, but it wasn't about us, it was his family and what they were facing.'

The photograph of Nicky with Bob in the winners' enclosure shows him pulling Bob's ear, like a playful punch on the arm. Bob was a thoroughly good sort, and as Nicky says, 'There was nothing flashy, he would never have told you he was a Gold Cup winner at any stage of his life.'

Bob also picked up the Lexus at Leopardstown, with Barry's family there to cheer him on his home turf, Lois in the crowd, and the commentator announcing, 'we have a Gold Cup winner'. 'It was huge for the Lexus, huge for Bob, huge for all of us,' says Kimbo. 'Every race he won was mind-boggling for us, we couldn't believe what was happening.'

When Bob returned to the Festival to defend his Gold Cup title, he was fifth to a quite staggering run by Lord Windermere and Davy Russell, who went from being detached, not even slightly in contention, and hanging badly right, to clinching it, and Bob was only beaten by four lengths and that's just because 'he jumped the last and ducked left and we think he wanted to go round again!' Kimbo says, his deep affection for Bob clear.

After a few disappointing runs over fences, Nicky decided to put him back over hurdles. He took on Simonsig at Aintree with Nicky's emerging star Nico de Boinville, jumped upsides him at the last and pushed Simonsig into second. 'It was miles too short for Bob, and perfect for Simonsig, since he won the Arkle. Everyone assumed he'd beat Bob, but it was the other way round,' says Nicky.

'I was using the race to get them to the next step and it suited them perfectly for what I was trying to do. I expected Simonsig to win but that was Bob, he would always floor you, that's the sort of person he was, he never stopped surprising you.'

It was decided with happiness that his final run would be back at Cheltenham for the World Hurdle. He was third to Thistlecrack and was, as Kimbo says, 'very brave and took on a lot of good horses'. He had endeared himself to the public with his honest decency and good bloke-ness. As Barry says, 'His character and demeanour attracted a lot of followers, he was owned by a small syndicate, it was a low-key affair and he was such an achiever.'

When Bob hung up his racing plates, there was only one place that he should spend his retirement.

* * *

Around 3,000 horses retire from racing annually, but there's no official traceable record of what happens to them. Di Arbuthnot, former head of the Retraining of Racehorses charity, ROR, wants to change that and 'help and persuade owners they do need to take some responsibility, not all through a horse's life but certainly the first stage. Sending them to a bloodstock sale is perfectly responsible, but, if not, try and find a home or retraining organisation to give a start for a second career.'

'That would be great' says Nicky, 'but lots of people who have racehorses aren't necessarily horsey people, have never ridden, and they love the racing but wouldn't know what to do.' So instead, he feels that it falls to the trainer. 'We must be the ones who are responsible.' To that end, any that are unsafe, unsound or tricky can have a life in the field at Seven Barrows. For the others, 'they are nearly always given away, not sold; all racehorses are registered with Wetherby's, and the new owners sign a piece of paper to say they will never sell or race the horse and if for any reason they can't cope, ring me and we'll take him back – and we have done, and rehoused them'.

* * *

Bob had spent all of his summer holidays at the nearby stud farm, run by Tracy and Charlie Vigors and their growing family, (they now have two sons, Harry and Oliver) and he had taken a fancy to one person in particular from the very start. Tracy says, 'When Harry was in his pram parked outside the stables when we were working, he was always the one that Bob would take a big interest in, and Harry was feeding him carrots and apples as a little toddler before he could walk … so it was always Bob.'

Nicky remembers, 'You knew he was safe, he was the only horse that Tracy's boys could lead out of the field.' On one of Harry's early birthdays, Nicky bought Bob's colours for him to wear while he posed for beaming photos on Bob. Harry and Oliver made him birthday cakes (special guest to one of the parties on 21 May: Nicky) and sat on the grass with him, near his steel shod hooves and in no danger whatsoever while he grazed around them. He was Harry's best friend and Harry happily, safely, rode Bob around the school.

When hacking out, Bob was ridden by Tracy's husband Charlie, and she says he might buck or squeal, to let everyone know he was having fun and 'keep Charlie on his toes'. Like any horse, he had his own unknowable code: traffic, tractors and farm machinery were no problem, but if he came across daffodils, he'd pull a cartoonish double take, every time, and give a signal that he would need to make a safe, but dramatic detour. He took everything in his stride, accompanying ponies on lead reins, staying out of trouble in his paddock, and taking to hunting in a major way. Tracy says, 'He'd

139

get a little bit excited when he got to the meet, he absolutely loved it, and stood still and majestic while the ponies were messing around. He didn't have to be in front, he was happy to fit in.' In Tracy's photographs, this horse who was considered small and rather unimposing on a racecourse absolutely bloomed in retirement.

Tracy says he had the sweetest nature, with never a single moment of being fed up, no ears back, no nips, not a foot stamp, or an angry swish of the tail. He was more than a pleasure, she describes him as 'very, very good for the soul'. Lois says, 'His whole life was in clover, he was a very lucky horse.' Barry received a constant stream of photos and video and says, 'He was living the most beautiful life with such a great family, he was so loved.' Lois and the syndicate owners, by now firm friends and brought together by the joy of being involved with this horse, met every year for lunch in the local pub before visiting the elder statesman himself.

Lois was a lifelong rider and one year, she remembers, 'Tracy and Charlie had him looking beautiful and Charlie was riding. When he got off, I said, "Gosh, I'd love to sit on him."' She had always regretted that she'd never been on his back, having bred, him, cared for him, seen him being sold, watched him racing and celebrated his wins, and it was a missing piece of the puzzle.

Up you get, said Charlie. 'To ride him, it closed the book and finished the story. I'd done everything,' Lois says. 'It's a chance not many breeders get, especially when horses go to England, you rarely get the chance of meeting the owners, let alone being there, throughout his wonderful life.' If not for the photos that surround her and the trophies for top breeder that Bob won for her, she says she'd wonder if it was all a dream.

Bob had six years as the adored fifth member of the Vigors family, and then catastrophe struck when he broke his leg in the field, aged 17 on 20 January 2022. Tracy describes her mounting unease as she went to collect him from the field and he didn't come to the gate as usual. He was 'standing with his head down, saying "help me".' Charlie and Tracy have no idea how it happened. They called the vet immediately, who said it didn't appear to be a kick, and suggested that he may have slipped. It was a freak accident, and there was nothing that could be done to save him. They were distraught.

Charlie called Nicky to break the news. When Nicky rang Barry to tell him what had happened, 'we both shed a tear', Barry says, for a horse 'so gorgeous, such a kind-natured individual and living the life he deserved. It's sad for Bob and the boys especially, they looked after him so well, it was a lovely thing to witness.' Nicky says, 'He loved life from the very beginning to the very end, he just should have had another ten years.' Kimbo was totally heartbroken and says, 'The worst thing that ever happened to us was to lose him. It was the most devastating call I've ever had in my life, and that applies to all of us, to hear that Bob had to be put down. I couldn't believe it, it was devastating, and I still can't believe it.'

Tracy posted a message on social media to let his devoted fans know and added a tribute. 'Blessed to have had you as our best friend Bob … you taught my family kindness, love and respect and I am so truly grateful forever. We are broken and empty without you and miss you so much. We will never forget you.'

She says now, 'He had something about him that made you want to love him and respect him.' She remembers when Harry went hunting on his pony, Charlie on Bob, they'd come back wet, cold, and tired, and always looked after the horses first: prepare the mash, take the plaits out, wash their legs in the freezing cold. 'The horses come first,' she says, but even after that, 'there was something about Bob, once you'd finished, you still didn't want to leave him.'

Her breath still catches when she says, 'It's hard to explain … he was lovable, that's what he was, and when Harry came into the yard, Bob was over the stable door with a kind eye. When Harry broke his arm, he was back from hospital and straight off to Bob. He was Harry's soulmate and Charlie hasn't ridden since. We miss him so much, that's the problem. He was so special.'

9

SIMONSIG

The shy Arkle-winning grey, devoted to chestnut chaser Triolo D'Alene

SIMONSIG GAVE his owner, Ronnie Bartlett, a preview of the fun he'd be delivering when he ran in the 2011 £100,000 bumper at Fairyhouse, sponsored by the brothers O'Leary's Gigginstown House Stud. Jockey Chris Cully was told nothing more than to let the horse go when he got inside the last three furlongs, and in a field of 16, he went off as favourite and beat Kandinski into second by an emphatic 13 lengths. The prize money was for the first four home, but traditionally, Michael O'Leary also offered a £100,000 bonus if he could buy the horse on the day. Ronnie remembers, 'The horse duly won, great banter, we got presented with the trophy and one of the people from Fairyhouse came up to me and said, "Ronnie, you know the offer from Michael O'Leary. Is it deal or no deal?" I said, "Put another zero on it and we'll think about it!"'

'Ronnie was never selling him,' Ian Ferguson, Simonsig's first trainer says, 'he thought it was wonderful to win a bumper with him.' Nicky was at Fairyhouse that day and Ronnie told him he'd be sending this horse to him in a few weeks' time. 'He was always going to Nicky, he was never going anywhere else. I think he's a Nicky type of horse,' he says, 'the style of horse he keeps buying.'

Nicky saw that Simonsig 'won by a million miles that day. He was by the most unfashionable sire in England or Ireland there ever was, Fair Mix, God bless him.' He may have been as out of date as smoking on an aeroplane, but the shot hit the target, and Simonsig was the best he produced, by any metric. The most wins, as a percentage (62 per cent) or as a total, the biggest total earnings (£267,724, in second place Cool Mix with £83,006), the best official rating according to the BHA (160), the best Racing Post Rating (167). 'The horse didn't surprise me but his breeding did,' Ian says. He was not necessarily good on paper, as Ian notes with all his decades of experience, but that's where the spark comes in: 'These good ones have a bit of a freak in them, I don't care what way they're bred, they just have that edge.'

Ian had seen what Simonsig could do, from the first time the three-year-old stretched his legs on the gallops. 'I was going to give the young lad a right bollocking for giving him a squeeze,' he remembers, 'I don't like the young horses to be under pressure, but he came back to me and before I could say anything he said, "I promise you, boss, I didn't move a muscle, he did that of his own accord." He didn't seem to be out of third gear.'

Horses at that stage in their careers are often trained to win a point-to-point in the spring, before going to the sales, so there's pressure for a win, to attract high bidders. That wasn't the case here, at all. 'The beauty with Ian is that he wasn't preparing him for the sales,' Nicky explains, 'he was prepping them for the future for Ronnie Bartlett who already owned him, so there was no pressure to win and he didn't have to drill the horse to get him ready for the time he gets to me in the summer.' In short, when Simonsig arrived, 'his mind was good because he'd been minded'.

Ian responds, 'That's very kind ... the horse was pretty straightforward, chilled out, never any trouble, just wonderful, and we didn't rush him.' Soaring potential in plain sight, but an unhurried trainer needs a forbearing owner and Simonsig's owners, originally Simon Tindall and then Ronnie Bartlett, were both as patient as wildlife photographers, so Ian could instead take his instructions from the horse, and arrive at the racecourse 'when the horse told me he was ready to run as opposed to having an owner who was very anxious to have a runner'. How did he say he was ready? 'When you've been at this for 50-odd years you get a message,' he says and can't be any clearer than that. That's trainers for you. And horsemen. You know or you don't. The ability to read a horse, to communicate with them, can't be taught. Ronnie says, 'I don't have much patience in business but with horses you've got to have patience, it's frustrating and disappointing but that's the way it is, there's no point going too quick or running them if they're not right, you'll only end up with another problem.'

Simonsig was right, and when he arrived at Seven Barrows, he started making waves. His jockey Barry Geraghty remembers vividly his first impressions of this seriously good grey. 'The things that stood out when I first rode him were one: how impressively he did it, and two: how much of a shell he was; he was so raw and immature and to put in the performance he put in, being so physically immature, showed so much potential. When you're first jockey at Seven Barrows and you have a conveyor belt of quality horses, it's frightening to think this is the norm: Simonsig, Sprinter Sacre, Finian's Rainbow. Exciting horses.'

Dave Fehily rode him day to day and says, 'He wasn't the easiest to ride, he was quite headstrong, his own worst enemy, not unrideable but keen to get on with things. He wouldn't take off but he'd test you.' Corky thought he was wonderful, and frequently told another lad, James Nixon, that he was the best horse they'd ever see, the horse of their lifetime.

He won his first race for Nicky by 11 lengths at Ascot – Brass Tax was second – and come the 2012 Cheltenham Festival he lined up for the Neptune Novices' Hurdle with Barry on board.

* * *

It was a twist of fate that led Barry to Seven Barrows. In 2008, he'd been due to ride Catch Me in the Champion Hurdle, but part-owner Paddy Monaghan decided Barry 'just wasn't lucky' for him, so he lost the ride (Ruby Walsh picked it up) and at the last minute, Barry was offered Nicky's Punjabi for the same race. He ran gallantly to third place (Catch Me was sixth). Punjabi and Barry won the Champion Hurdle at Punchestown a month later in April 2008 and after a Minty-arranged talk, Barry came to work for Nicky.

Now, Barry can look back and say, 'Paddy was a good friend but he was taking no prisoners. I met him a couple of years later and I wouldn't have looked fondly on him after the Catch Me incident, but he said I should thank him. I was taken aback, but he said, "You wouldn't have got the job with Nicky if not for this."'

Barry stayed with Nicky and Sophie for his first year and says, 'He was a brilliant housemate, it was always an open house. We had a few late nights,' but Nicky's attention to detail never waned once in all the years that Barry worked for (and lived with) him. He remembers, 'First lot was 7.30am and I'd call into the office at 7.15. I'd never once be in the office before him, and when I came in, he'd checked all the gallops for frost, read the paper, studied the form, he could tell you anything that's going to happen that day. That's the level of commitment he has, and ambition, but not at a price.'

For Barry, living on site (the stables are *right there* outside the back door, around a grass square like a stately home for horses), 'We were like-minded in our approach, doing things for the right reasons, not just for the win. The horse will come first and that's one of the best things about riding for Nicky.' As proof, he says, come the end of the season there is all to play for and 'you don't see him run horses that are ready for the field, you won't see him run a horse for the trainer's title, he'll do what's right for the horse. If it's right to run, brilliant, but he won't unless it's right and it could be the difference between being champion trainer or not. It's so far from the win-at-all-costs attitude and the horses benefit from that longer term.'

* * *

Come the parade ring, for the Neptune Novices' Hurdle in March 2012, Barry knew Simonsig inside out, as he did all of the horses he rode at Seven Barrows. 'We'd discussed them through the season, on previous runs, learned about them, what to do and not to do, constantly gathering information and the same regarding the opposition, filling your book with details,' like detectives painstakingly putting a case together. It was second nature, knowing 'what the team want to do, what the opposition will do, what's your trump card, how will you get the best out of your horse and beat them all to the winner's enclosure'.

The information wasn't wasted, Simonsig won it 'at a canter', seeing off 16 other contenders, pushing Cheltenham rival Willie Mullins's trained Felix Yonger into a seven lengths second place.

It may have looked easy, but it never is, not least for the connections. Ronnie watched it all unfold from the paddock, and as they were coming round the last bend, going away from the field, he wondered, is this really happening? It was Ronnie's first Grade One win: 'We didn't know how good the horse was when we bought him but we knew we had something special after he won the flat race at Fairyhouse, but his authority when he won the Neptune, we had to pinch ourselves. Is this real?'

It was, and it was so spectacular that he says, 'If he never won another race after that, he'd done enough.' But Simonsig wasn't nearly finished.

He also won all but one of his hurdle races, finishing that part of his career with a swan-song spectacular, 15-length win at Aintree over Super Duty, before turning his firepower to fences. He won his Novices' Chase at Ascot by an enormous 49 lengths from Sulpius, 35 lengths separated him and the second place Hinterland at Kempton for the December 2012 Novices' Chase, then came the Arkle in March 2013, the Grade One two-mile chase.

It was a battle for this phenomenal athlete, and he won despite being quite significantly under the weather, as was discovered after the race. A scope (in which vets use an endoscope to see a horse's airways or stomach lining) revealed he rated 4/5 for mucus and blood. Barry says, 'A good horse will find a way to win; he shouldn't have won as he was so unhealthy, as it transpired.' He blundered at the ninth fence and had to work much harder than he should but 'he had the edge of class; quality is the thing that'll win it for you. I just had to hang on to him, keep conserving, that'll get him home and it did.' Ronnie agrees that 'I think that tells you about the horse.' It was Dave's proudest moment too: 'He was such a good jumper, so clever, a bit keen but he knew what he was doing.'

Nicky says, 'He won the Neptune and an Arkle and to most that would be fantastic but we all knew we hadn't seen the best of him. He was a huge talent with a great will to win, but he was very hard to train.' Unlike See You Then, who had one major problem with his tendons, Simonsig was delicate and could go wrong anywhere. 'He was desperately fragile, with poor bone structure, his whole constitution was fragile, his lungs were not great, he had splints and was always getting issues,' Nicky says. 'Some are tough structurally, however badly you train, you'll never break down an ordinary horse because they don't go fast enough. The good horses go faster and the faster you go the more problems you'll get.'

* * *

It is supernatural what racehorses can do. Horses store red blood cells in their spleen, which sits on the left-hand side of the abdomen. Equine sports medicine specialist Kate Allen, explains, 'When at rest, chilled out or walking, probably 40 per cent of their blood is made up of red blood cells, but when they start doing strenuous exercise, what is pretty unique to them is that they can quite quickly contract their spleen and then they dump a whole load of extra red blood cells into the circulating blood stream, so up to 60 per cent of circulating blood is made up of red blood cells. After exercise it goes back into the spleen and gets stored. The red blood cells take oxygen from the lungs to the muscles and the only way for muscles to work for any period of time is to have oxygen, so it's a really incredible oxygen delivery system when compared to other species. All horses could do it, from a biological point, but they probably don't need to, so it's most studied and understood in the racehorse.'

When walking or trotting, horses breathe whenever they choose, but once cantering or galloping, they change to 'locomotor respiratory coupling' and take one breath for every stride. At one point on a racing gallop, the horse's entire weight (around 500kg) is borne on one foot. When they take off over a fence, there is a point where they lose sight of it in their blind spot directly in front, due to the position of their eyes (they have a blind spot behind too). When they land over a jump at speed, the force of approximately two-and-a-half times their body weight (about the weight of a Mini) goes through their non-leading front leg. Kate says, 'Everything we ask them to do is brave. It's phenomenal what we ask of them and how willing they are to do it.'

* * *

Corky knew Simonsig was talented, but says, 'He was always a bit hyper riding out, a bit strange, there was something about him. He was hard to settle, nervy, panicky with his head in the air running away, he didn't help himself, didn't give himself a chance.' When he was tucked in behind the others, he'd pull and fight, swing from side to side, so Corky told his work rider, jockey Jerry McGrath to 'let him make the running, settle him up front' instead. Dave Fehily looked after Simonsig and rode him day to day. He noticed who he was in his quiet time and says he was 'a very shy horse, not very sociable, always to the back of the box, never in your face, he always liked his own space'.

After the Arkle, Simonsig had problems with splints for two years, an eternity in the life of any professional athlete, and Ronnie came to dread seeing Nicky's name on his phone, delivering more bad news. They were close friends, year-round, and Ronnie says, 'The passion he speaks with, it's like a death in the family for him when he says the horse isn't right again. It's equally as frustrating for him as it is for us.'

Nicky says there are tough times every single day, ringing the owner to say 'we've got a problem, it's a year off, retire him, the game's up … it's horrible and we face it every day.'

When Charlie Mann was training, he'd time these calls for 11am, in the hope the owner was busy and important in their air-conditioned corner office somewhere, and not really concentrating on his call. He had a tot of whisky too. He describes horses as accidents waiting to happen, and remembers the intense frustration as a trainer of a) having a horse good enough to run in the Gold

Cup and b) that same horse treading on a stone two days before the Gold Cup. Every single element of the horse's prep had been geared towards this race, and just like that, he was out and Charlie had another difficult call to make.

* * *

Come the summer holidays at the Vigorses' stud farm, ten or more horses would share a field, staying out all night like unruly teens, and loafing all day. One summer, there were eight bays including everybody's friend Bobs Worth, one grey (Simonsig) and one chestnut (Triolo d'Alene).

As thoroughbreds in the condition of their lives, with energy fizzing through their veins, to keep everyone safe, they are lightly sedated before they're let loose because 'if you turn ten out in a 50-acre field they will career around like lunatics', says Nicky, and they haven't had as much dinner as they usually would, so when they're let go, they immediately start grazing, and gradually wake up.

'It's the most lovely sight,' says Nicky, still charmed by it after all these years, 'suddenly they're on holiday, back shoes off, sometimes front too, like kids home from school. The excitement! They don't know it's going to happen the day before and they find themselves in a great field of lush grass. I'm allowed to do what I want! I can gallop! It's a joy, the sedation wears off and I'm free! Suddenly they realise and have a right good spin around, heads down.'

Every year, the horses gathered into their two separate groups. 'I don't know if the eight bays wouldn't have them,' Nicky says, 'but Triolo and Simon lived together in this field, the bays at one end and these two always on their own at the other end of the field, from day one, like they'd been ostracised. It was an extraordinary situation. It had to be to do with their colour – a bright chestnut and a light grey – then for a year they wouldn't see each other, then they were turned out, the same thing, the two and the eight. They went off together, and wherever you went, there were eight bays and those two in the corner, they never went near the others and every year it was the same. They were brothers.'

Tracy Vigors describes Simonsig as shy, always standing at the back of his stable though over time, he relaxed a little. Perhaps it was falling for Triolo that did it. 'It was a proper love affair,' she says, 'I've never seen anything like it. They'd drink from the same water trough, eat from the same feed manger and parallel walk across the field. They were always together.'

When Simonsig and Triolo returned to Seven Barrows, they carried on their inseparable romance, living in the covered ride together one year, and in boxes with half height walls another. They even kept their back shoes on.

Helen Stevens, who looked after Triolo d'Alene remembers visiting the lovebirds too. 'Simon was quite nervy and Trio was the coolest, gentlest horse and, I don't know, Simonsig felt safeguarded by him.' She's never seen a bond like it: 'Horses have attachments, but to be so faithful? Every summer, and together in open stables so they could talk over the wall?

'They were each other's safety blankets,' she says. Triolo arrived as a gangly four-year-old, and 'on the first day Ben Pauling rode him – you never know what you're going to get – he said, "I think you've got a nice one here Helen." There was no malice in Triolo, I rode him every day, he was a happy horse. Simon was a bit scatty, a lot of nervous energy.'

There's no doubt that horses remember each other. Research has shown they are able to recognise and remember whinnies of herd members and distinguish them from whinnies of horses they don't know. A University of Sussex study led by Dr Karen McComb took familiar members of a horse's herd past them and away, out of sight. The horses were then played a recorded whinny from a different horse than the one they'd just seen. They were startled, their response was quicker, and they looked in the direction of the whinny for longer. It was an 'expectancy violation', the whinny didn't match with the horse they knew.

* * *

After their summer of love, the horses returned to their day jobs. Simonsig went back over hurdles in November 2015, beaten into a surprising second at Aintree by the ever-gallant Bobs Worth, and a few lacklustre performances later, he was ready to line up again in November 2016 at Cheltenham for the Grade Two Shloer Chase. Earlier in the day, Nicky had held a press conference to announce Sprinter Sacre's retirement, which may sound dramatic but there was only one way for a once-in-a-lifetime superstar to bow out. He was never going to leave the stage quietly and the horse paraded in front of the stands to allow everyone's spines to tingle once more. Nicky spilled a few tears of happiness, that this horse's spellbinding career had come to an end. Minutes later, absolute devastation and tears of deep unsayable sorrow.

Simonsig stumbled at the first, and for the first time running under Rules, he fell, at the third, and was fatally injured. Commentator Simon Holt remembers saying something as sensitive as he could (the days of hearing words like 'broken leg' over the tannoy are long gone) and offered, 'I'm sorry to say unfortunately he looks to be injured.'

Barry was riding and remembers the heart-stopping moment. 'I got him caught and got him at ease as much as you can. You want to be there for them, but you don't want to be there for that moment either. I stepped away and gave him to the vet at the last second,' he recalls. He was so precious to so many, a superstar and 'we all loved him to bits; his owners Ronnie and Freda are the nicest people in the world and so patient throughout. We eventually get him to Cheltenham to a race and we're all looking forward to it and – boom – this happens. It was devastating for everyone, he was a gorgeous, special horse owned by the best people, it was desperate,' Barry recalls.

'It's quiet,' Nicky says of the atmosphere at the time, 'and everybody respects you for it in a way. Ronnie didn't need to talk to me, I didn't need to talk to him. We're the best of mates and he's the most lovely man in the world, and it broke his heart. He knows it broke ours, we broke each other's hearts, we didn't need to say anything. We're all too emotional anyway, I'm sure you've learned that.' He sums it up by saying simply, 'You're meant to be bringing the horse back.'

The change in the atmosphere is extraordinary, tens of thousands of people affected by the loss of one of nature's best. 'People call out, but you're in your own little world, on good and bad days in a funny way. You don't know who you're feeling sorry for, for yourself, but more than anything whoever looks after the horse. One person looks after three horses, and they live for them. They're more important to me than the owner at that time, they look after that horse day in and day out, seven days a week; the horse is like a child or husband or wife to them.

'For the owner, it's his pride and joy, and however good or moderate – there's no such thing as a bad horse – you know it hurts somebody who looks after them. They're devastated and every single horse is as important as another. It's crippling when you lose a real superstar but it's just as bad when you lose an ordinary one, it has the same effect down the line. That horse has his person that looks after him, feeds him morning and night, mucks the box out, puts him to bed, wakes him up every morning, feeds, cleans, rides, looks after him immaculately. They are the ones carrying the empty saddle and bridle home; you take the bridle off the horse and take it back. It's horrendous, going home to an empty horse-box and waking up to an empty box. It's the owner's horse, not ours, but it's the people who look after them that are our first port, that's the person it hits the hardest and it's the toughest part of it.'

Helen says 'It's gut-wrenching, heartbreaking for the whole stable, it doesn't matter who it is, if it's a horse you're not connected to, it was someone's love, they are all like our little pets.'

Ronnie was there and says, 'You felt numb, just numb, it was like a bad dream, over before it started. You don't think it could happen with a horse like that but it did.' He gallantly says, 'It's for everybody, not just the jockey or the owner, it's the staff at Nicky's from Corky down, involved in mending him and trying to get him to the racecourse, the hours that people tried, they are the unsung heroes.'

It's a private, devastating loss, all played out in public and as swiftly as possible for the sake of the horse. Walking back, alone, up the horse walk, with an empty and still warm bridle, saliva still on the bit, flecks of mud on the browband in the horse's glamorous colours, the saddle cloth still warm and damp with sweat, all remnants of the aliveness, and no horse, no horse, to carefully take home.

* * *

It's a loss that cuts very deep. Corky remembers when he lost his beloved Killiney at Fred's yard. He was a horse of thrilling talent and potential, the English Arkle. When Corky's wife Diane once rang the bookies to see if he'd won, the bookie said, 'Don't you mean how much did he win by?' When he was fatally injured and put down at the races, Corky was completely undone by it. Fred visited him that night, with a bottle of the strong stuff. 'He said, "Come back next week, next month or next year, but don't give up the game, it's a lovely game and you're good at it." I said, "OK guv'nor.' Corky returned to the yard two days later. There was no horse in the box, just an awful stillness, and the top door was bolted shut for weeks. 'Then I saw the top door open, it was time. I've never forgotten that; it was 56 years ago,' he says.

Charlie Mann has retired from training and remembers in his last season he lost three horses and 'it doesn't get any easier, It's distressing, you're in bits. I've held horses on the gallops that have broken a back leg and you feel so helpless. I had a lovely mare, looking at me, saying, can you help me? Waiting for a vet breaks you and it never gets any easier.' He remembers a horse winning at Fakenham in his last year of training, and 15 lengths clear he broke his shoulder at the last. Charlie had to stop in a lay-by on the way back and ring the syndicate owners to give them the devastating news. 'I had to make that call 12 times and it literally breaks you. it's hard enough to make one call. Horses all have different characters, they're all people and it's heartbreaking.'

Chris Jerdin (CJ) worked for Nicky's great friend Oliver Sherwood for nearly 30 years and looked after the late Many Clouds from day one. After landing the Hennessy Gold Cup in 2014 and the Grand National in 2015, Clouds became a celebrity, accepting fruit baskets and visits from fans 'including two nuns from Ireland, they knew quite a lot about racing actually,' CJ says. He loved sharing this horse, the love of his life. On 28 January 2017, catastrophe came when Clouds collapsed and died on the Cheltenham turf, having just beaten the favourite Thistlecrack in a hard-won Cotswold Chase, ridden by his only jockey Leighton Aspell. As they passed the post, CJ ran after him, then saw him go down. He stood behind the dreaded green screens right in front of the packed stands, with four or five vets and Leighton, holding his saddle. 'He said, "He's gone, CJ" and they left me alone,' he remembers, 'I wish I'd knelt down and patted him but I was so upset I left.' Instead of leading him back to the winner's enclosure, CJ walked the same horse-walk, alone, to a pin-drop quiet crowd. 'There are 70,000 people watching, but you're the loneliest person going back to the stables. It was terrible … terrible. I was numb. I could hear sobbing over the tannoy. The gate people couldn't say anything. What could they say? Saying nothing meant they knew what it meant. Coming home with the empty box was terrible. You never get used to it and if you do, you shouldn't be doing it.' CJ still goes to the yard every Saturday to polish the plaques that Clouds won as Horse of the Year.

Simon Knapp, racecourse veterinary surgeon, says the standard of racecourse vetting has improved immensely; vets go on training courses for continuing education every five years, there are fracture support kits at every racecourse for immediate support, specialist ambulances and state of the art equine hospitals. He says, 'Losing a horse is horrific. It's always sad, nobody ever thinks it's acceptable, every loss hurts but we are doing much more to get them back. They may not race again, but they can have a good lifestyle elsewhere.' On a race day, they always debrief at the end of the day and 'that's when emotion comes out, and if it doesn't, we're in the wrong job. Every horse matters, whatever the quality of horse or standard of race, they all get same treatment.'

He talks of looking over the stable door at a horse and 'how privileged we are to be involved with these magnificent animals. If people don't feel a passion for the horse, and emotional when it goes wrong, they're in the wrong job. The emotion is very raw in the debrief – tears – and the longer you're at it, the more you know the horses, makes it worse. We shouldn't be ashamed to cry, it's not a macho world and I've seen Nicky in tears many times.' It's a courageous sport, full of daily derring-do, but talk to anyone in racing about their favourite horse and you'll hear an unmistakable sweetness that will stop you in your tracks.

* * *

Ronnie says now, 'You've got to remember the good days, because you have more bad days than good and you don't want to get used to that feeling, so you've got to make sure you enjoy the good days.'

It casts a pall; Barry says it's hard for any jockey to leave a horse behind the screens, walk alone back to the weighing room, take off the silks, and somehow be ready to give the next horse every chance to run its best race. It's bearable, he says, because that horse deserves their shot at glory, and because race-riding doesn't leave any room for thinking about the past or the future, it's a sort of maniacal mindfulness, at a steady 30mph. Barry says, 'Once you're on the track, because racing is so demanding, it's completely consuming, no matter what's on your mind, there's only one thing on your mind in a race. It takes all of your attention; you read of people who have demons [but who] are most at peace in the heat of that moment.'

There was one more dagger through the heart to come. 'I will never forget the night Simonsig went off to the races,' Nicky says, 'Triolo was there, he knew he was going in the horse-box, he knew he'd gone racing and he was in his box waiting for Simonsig to come home. When the horse-box came back, I went down the drive as I wanted to see Dave, who looked after Simonsig. As the box came up, Triolo started whinnying because he knew it was bringing his mate back, he whinnied all the way up the drive and Simonsig didn't come back.'

Helen had left Nicky's yard by the time of Simonsig's fall. When she heard, her first thought was 'Oh my poor boy, waiting for him.'

* * *

As if the body blow of returning without Simonsig wasn't intense enough, there was the extra pain of Triolo. 'You didn't know what to feel,' Nicky says, 'but you just knew this horse had lost his partner. There was such telepathy between these two, I wondered how much it affected him. He knew he'd set off in the morning and he didn't come back. It took him time, it took us all time, it always does, it's horrible. Triolo had lost his complete soulmate, they lived together for three years and summered for four, it was an extraordinary thing. It's hard to understand how a horse would comprehend something like that, it's always something I thought about. Triolo was the easiest horse you'll ever train, a good staying chaser, a galloper, Simonsig was a fast, fast horse and they were married. He cried for him: where is he? He thought he was coming back, his whinnying was extraordinary. We were in a bad enough way, Ronnie and Dave, it was horrendous for everybody, I almost felt more sorry for Triolo than I did Dave. Dave was devastated.'

Dave remembers leading him up at Cheltenham. He had high hopes for his shy friend, it was the ideal race for him; Grade Two, two miles. Playing to his strengths, it was a race made for him. When he fell, Dave says, 'It's just horrendous really, something you don't want to go through again.' He saw it happen, and he rushed down to the course with Sophie, and 'I met Barry and he just said it was bad news. That was it really.' Dave didn't get the chance to go behind the dreaded green screens, he couldn't bear to see him like that. 'He was such a nice person, wouldn't harm anyone, very quiet at home. It was the worst day in racing I had.'

Everyone felt it at Seven Barrows. As for Triolo? 'I couldn't say he died of a broken heart,' Nicky says, 'but you could say he probably wasn't as good again. He'd already been a good horse by then, he had a long and happy retirement, which Simonsig never did get.' And these are the losses that everyone absorbs.

10

SPRINTER SACRE

The charismatic chaser who raised the roof with racing's greatest comeback

SPRINTER SACRE always behaved like a superstar, way before he was one, as stable lad James Nixon knows well. He led Sprinter up for his first race, a bumper at Ascot, before he became *the* Sprinter. Even in those early days, it was like trying to keep hold of an untethered hot air balloon. He remembers, 'We had to bring him up early, he was wailing [full of himself] round the pre-parade, he looked a million dollars, and he went nuts every time horses came past him. He was so naughty in the paddock; honestly, I thought he'd get lapped a few times. He was pretty excited, I thought he's either going to get loose or blow his top before we even get onto the course. He knew he was there for that reason; he looked the best, he made sure people knew he was there: look at me, I can do this. He was just a diamond. Leading him in after his first win – his first run – he was snorting like a stallion.'

Barry Geraghty remembers it too; Sprinter already had a reputation. 'I hadn't really met him before the parade ring. I got up, he was gorgeous and amazing and travelled well through the race. There'd been so much talk beforehand, when we knuckled down, I had to get stuck in to beat Ruby a short head. He'd have heard all the talk and was telling me, "I hear this is a machine." Sprinter gave me a little fright that day, but he learned so much and improved so much. Then he went to Ayr on Scottish National day, and destroyed the field. He's one of most impressive I ever sat on in a bumper, he blew the roof off.'

'Sprinter Sacre took us to places, heart-string wise, that no other horse ever had,' Nicky says. 'He had a profound effect on people, just to see him.' He created specialness and changed the atmosphere wherever he went; and he knew it. He sensed the power of his own presence, from the moment he entered the parade ring and danced on hot coals around it.

And all of this from a horse who arrived purely by chance and with no fanfare to Seven Barrows. He'd been part of a job lot of 22 horses picked up from a closing French yard, £300,000 for all of them.

Minty remembers the random way it all started. In 2007, he heard that French trainer Robert Fougedoire was selling his horses due to ill health and he sprang into action. From 9am on a Saturday morning, streams of fax paper curled out of the machine and spread like a rising tide on the floor detailing pedigrees, and Minty cut them up, and picked five or six of the best. To his shock, owner and pal, the late Raymond Mould, suggested that they buy them all and 'everyone fell off their chairs and within half an hour the deal was done'. The vet Buffy Shirley-Beavan hopped onto a ferry, sped to the horses and in four hours vetted, scoped and led up all the horses; one failed the tests, but within eight days the horses were bought, paid for, and shipped to Minty's yard the following Monday. It was, he says, quite extraordinary. The plan was to sell some and keep some but one morning in 2009 when they'd all developed, Raymond said, 'Let's train them all, they'll run in my wife's name – and send those three bays to Nicky.' Just like that. Sprinter was one of the trio, and, 'I couldn't say he was outstanding,' Minty says now, 'he blossomed in life, the better he got, the more stature.'

161

Caroline, Raymond's wife says, 'I chose him, I picked him from the ones left, he was just a baby.' She knew a little about it all, but as he became the horse of a lifetime, so entirely other, she felt unworthy, an imposter: 'If you're pretty green, like me, I felt a fake, I hadn't been involved that long, how did I chose that horse?' He went into training and she thought no more of it until Nicky called her and said, 'I think you've got something rather special,' but as ever, no one knows for sure until the hooves hit the turf.

He took to schooling in the same way that Remittance Man had done, and Altior would; the triumvirate of natural athletes. Nicky says, 'He took off outside the wings, the jockey might be expecting another stride, but taking off a stride too soon for most is curtains, they won't get there. For this one it didn't matter.' He was such a natural. 'We only schooled him twice a year, just to remind him where his feet are. Once before his first run. You just shut your eyes; like Altior, as soon as you turned them in to face the first fence they were gone, they loved it, they think it's terrific fun. Nico thought it was wonderful, for me it's the most frightening thing of the year; terrifying, far too fast, you can't stop them, and nothing else can go with them.'

It wasn't just the jumps either; he was so good on the gallops that only Simonsig could match him. It's not an option to 'use horses up as galloping companions' and sometimes other horses would relay; one would start in front of him and do the first five furlongs, and at the four-furlong marker, another, fresh horse would join in, take the lead as the first pulled up. The yard had to bend to his whims.

His hurdling career was a brisk stepping stone, mostly won on the bridle apart from one with AP McCoy, who says of that time, 'he had a wind problem and I tried to buy him afterwards, unsuccessfully, I offered quite a lot but it wasn't enough. It's hard to buy a horse with a wind problem that got beat, but I was stupid enough to try.' At least the wind operation went better than the offer.

In his debut over fences at Doncaster, he left the field 24 lengths behind, and then 16 lengths in the Novices' Chase at Kempton in December 2011. But from 17 February 2012 to 23 April 2013, it was Sprinter's race, Sprinter's era, Sprinter's world. Barry Geraghty rode him in every race of the season to end all seasons. At Newbury, he was on the bridle for the Grade Two Super Saturday Chase, as he was for his Grade One Arkle at the Festival and eased down in the closing stages, with Cue Card and Menorah in second and third, stars in any other competition than this. In the other Grade Ones: at Aintree for the Novices' Chase a month later, he was clear from two out and put 13 lengths between himself and Toubab; at the Tingle Creek at Sandown, he wasn't even extended by his 15-length victory over Kumbeshwar; was easily clear by 14 lengths in the Clarence House Steeple Chase; in the Queen Mother Champion Chase the magnificent Sizing Europe couldn't get any closer than 19 lengths; and then came the Melling Chase, still on the bridle two out, and Cue Card, Flemenstar, Finian's Rainbow and For Non Stop were only ever competing for second place. All that was left for the season was Punchestown; no horse had 'done the treble' – Cheltenham, Aintree, Punchestown – since Istabraq in 1999.

Sprinter was totally, thrillingly unbeatable, a glittering athlete beyond all athletes. 'It was hell for us,' Nicky says, 'because anything other than sheer brilliance was unacceptable. The rest of the world loved it. I hated it; all it could do was go wrong. Everybody expected him to fly round and win by ten minutes, that's what they had come to see. If he didn't (he always did) they were waiting for it to go wrong.'

It wasn't ungodly for everyone in Sprinter's inner circle. Barry, that most seasoned of big-occasion jump jockeys, says, 'It was a joy. There would be more pressure trying to beat him than there was trying to ride him.' (AP agrees, 'I like riding the favourite rather than trying to beat them, I'd pick the favourite every time, I'm shallow like that.')

The night before Sprinter was due to light up the turf, Caroline would call Barry. 'I was a bag of nerves. You're fine, until it hits you you've got 24 hours. I'd ask, "is everything going to be alright?"' 'Yes,' he always said. Caroline remembers, 'It was hell for Nicky understandably, I was just as bad. Barry was relaxed, but the jockey doesn't hear anybody in his bubble. As an owner I was very conscious of not wanting to put my anxiety onto the jockey or Nicky, but Barry is so level-headed, he'd come out cool as a cucumber, it was fascinating for me to talk to him.' Anxieties aside, she had 'huge faith in this horse, and I always did, like no other. He was beautiful, poetry in motion, just going to watch him was a privilege.'

Barry's only problem was to get him and keep him relaxed. 'He could make three lengths in the air, he could jump himself from fifth to first in a flash then he'd be set alight and he'd be gone, charging off in front with you, burning up the fuel. The key was to keep a lid on him, keep him relaxed and controlled and unleash that burst of speed when you really needed it. He had so much enthusiasm; I never rode a horse that left the ground and touched down the far side the way he did, he was unbelievable, he was so precise; don't think he ever even made a mistake, just such an athlete. He was a handful, if you could just control him to a small degree, he'd organise the rest and you could press the button for him to pick up at any point.'

Sprinter had swept all before him. The weekend before Punchestown, the course's racing manager Richie Galway found a man pacing the car park. He'd driven the 280-mile round trip, he told Richie, because, 'I have to come and see Sprinter Sacre, and I live in Cork, and I've never been here before and I don't know where to go.' 'Come with me', said Richie, who gave him a tour and two VIP tickets for what would be the day of days. 'In 50 years, I've never seen anything like it,' he says.

The ground was slower than they'd hoped and Richie rang Nicky a few days before, fearful that he might change his mind. 'No, we're committed, we're coming,' he said. The people needed to see this horse. When the horse-box arrived, anyone who could went to see him into the stable yard. 'He was a beautiful specimen and he looked to be a gent. I remember seeing him on the track the first morning, and it was a new environment to him and he took it all in his stride,' Richie recalls.

On the day itself, 23 April, people just wanted to shake Nicky's hand, to thank him for bringing Sprinter to Ireland. The President of Ireland, Michael D Higgins joined the record-breaking crowd of 18,607 to be in the presence of greatness. 'He came to thank connections for bringing him, to allow the Irish public to see him. It's not very often you get a horse that has that visual impact on a racetrack and attendance. There were crowds from all over the country, it was a huge opportunity for Irish racegoers to get the chance to see him in the flesh,' Richie says.

'I expect Sprinter knows he became an idol, an icon,' Caroline says. How could he not? He was lauded wherever he went, as Nicky says, 'He quadrupled the crowd, even the pre-parade in Ireland, and nobody ever goes there. It was mind boggling, wherever he went you could feel the atmosphere he was creating. He was a feisty beast, so he had earplugs to take the atmosphere out of it, so he couldn't appreciate it. I said, thank you, on his behalf, because he can't hear you, to the crowd.'

He was cheered into the parade ring before the race. Some racehorses prowl, some stalk, some lope, some saunter, but Sprinter bounces, he hears music. 'It was hectic,' Richie says, 'crowds five or six deep around the horse walk on the way out and as you walked down, the rails leaned into the middle of the horse exit because of the crush of people on both sides. Everyone was respectful but it was something we hadn't seen before. Davy Russell, on Noble Prince who came in fourth, said as we walked out to thousands of people trying to get a glimpse of him that he had never seen anything like that before.'

Barry remembers it vividly, 'The parade ring was ten deep, I've never witnessed anything like it. Cheltenham is amazing and massive but this was Sprinter Sacre's day, people travelled the length and breadth of Ireland because they longed to see this fella. It was a brilliant performance, and he was the first since Istabraq to win at all three festivals.

'I remember it all. Because it was Punchestown not Cheltenham, it was a swan-song for the season, and doing all he'd done, there was not the same level of pressure. It was a very rare thing, for me on a personal level, it was very special. I was able to enjoy it and soak it in and acknowledge people in the crowd and really appreciate the moment for what it was. We were cheered into the parade ring, clapped as we went round before the race, I've never seen anything like it, it was magic.'

The two-mile Grade One Champion Chase was, in theory, a five-horse race. Henry de Bromhead's Sizing Europe (last walloped by Sprinter in the seen-to-be-believed Champion Chase), Days Hotel, Noble Prince and Davy Russell, and Foildubh and Paul Carberry, all lined up with him.

Sprinter wasn't at his best that day (Nicky says he was at about 75 per cent), but then, he didn't need to be. Barry's MO was to try and keep a lid on him until he needed the overdrive, but jockeys always need Plan B, C and usually D. He remembers, 'Through the race he was unbelievable, down the back straight he was on springs, running away doing everything. We turned to the fourth last and hit a patch of heavy ground, it sucked the life out of him. I switched, hanging on and conserving, saving, just to get home. It was his will and guts that got him home. Sizing Europe didn't go to Aintree so he was a fresh horse and Sprinter Sacre had to dig deep. He answered every call, even at the last fence, meeting it on a really long stride; he was feeling the pinch but he came for me. It was a really solid performance, he was gutsy that day. Once he picked up at the last, it was the big one and when he left the ground, it was game over; you know when he picks up the touchdown is guaranteed.'

Sprinter wasn't used to scrapping; his races were usually an exhibition in elegance, breaking course records while cruising on the bridle with his motionless jockey occasionally looking behind to see how far away the rest of the field was, but he won by five-and-a-half lengths from Sizing Europe. His trainer Henry de Bromhead said with grace afterwards, 'At least we got your man off the bridle this time.' Nicky says that even though it all looked like it came easy for Sprinter, 'these horses … have to put a huge amount of mental and physical effort to do that. It looks easy but you can't beat those horses standing on your head.'

Cheered back into the parade ring, a French bred, English trained horse, coming to Ireland and stealing the show; has he considered a career in international diplomacy? All eyes on Sprinter, and it wasn't because he'd won the punters any money – at 1/9 odds – this was just thanking him for giving them the experience of wonder. Richie's been at Punchestown since 1998, and says, 'There are a handful of days that live in the memory, and that's as good as it got.'

Nicky was running out of races; Grade Ones are meant to be competitive. And commentators were running out of superlatives: 'scintillating … sparkling … spine-tingling'. How could he possibly follow this?

Come the Desert Orchid chase at Kempton on 27 December 2013, Barry remembers, he was quiet going to post. 'He wasn't tearing the arms out of my shoulders the way he would normally,' and once they got going, 'he wasn't giving me the same feel over fences, there was a spark that wasn't there. I was anxious not panicked, I remember giving him a squeeze before the second fence down the back; you don't need to go looking for strides on him, he just takes you there. Give him an inch – not even an inch – of rein and he lengthens and attacks fences. I was giving squeezes thinking, what's wrong here, and down the back, four, five strides before the seventh fence, I said this isn't right, and my mind was made up before we left the ground, I'd pull him up, I just knew this wasn't right.

'I was lucky in that position, and this goes back to Nicky, the horse comes first. My first instinct was, what's amiss? There's no benefit in me pressing any more buttons, there'd be a high likelihood of doing damage but also riding for the man I'm riding for, I can pull the horse up, come back and say "I don't know, but it wasn't happening," and if the horse pulled up perfectly fine, I wouldn't have had to explain myself. I knew I was meeting the right person coming back in. Caroline Mould is the same – she's a really good owner. It was an easy decision for me, I could do the right thing by the horse, be completely comfortable in the knowledge I wasn't going to get taken apart. That's the beauty of riding for Nicky.'

Barry's decades of experience also meant he could keep this in perspective, 'It was a shock but it wasn't the end of the road. Even in the moment, I was hopeful it was just a blip, he'll be OK later in the spring. [The death of] Simonsig was devastating; if Sprinter didn't race again, he was still OK.'

Sprinter was diagnosed with an irregular heartbeat, atrial fibrillation (AF). Esteemed Newmarket vet Celia Marr, RCVS and European veterinary specialist in equine internal medicine was called in. She explains that in a normal heart, a signal comes out of the pacemaker and spreads across the heart in a coordinated rhythmic fashion. AF means that the electrical signal which should travel across all the heart muscle in one solid wave has broken down and there is chaotic activity going on in the atria, the two top chambers in the heart. The job of the atria is to fill the heart. For any pump to work it has to be full, if you lose that coordinated activity from the filling chambers as the heart beats, it's not full enough to empty properly, and each heart beat releases a small amount of blood.

Racehorses have proportionately larger hearts than other breeds, 'It's one of the things that makes them superlative athletes,' Celia says, 'but with a larger heart there is more potential for it to lose coordination. Within the thoroughbred breed, the horses that have the biggest hearts tend to be top class National Hunt horses, where having a large heart helps for running fast over longer distances; it doesn't make a great deal of difference running five furlongs.'

AF happens instantaneously. Celia explains, 'The heart is beating normally then loses coordination suddenly, you never really know exactly the moment it happened. It could have been on the way to the start, it could have been during the race or even have been the night before. When a horse has AF, standing around or walking about it's not obvious externally, it's a problem only when they are asked to gallop. The other point about all horses – their hearts are much more efficient than they need to be to just walk about because their hearts are designed for athletic activity, so when not doing that, it can have quite a degree of compromise without it being at all apparent externally.'

Celia says it's like a car running out of petrol, 'The engine's gone, and the person that feels that first is the jockey. They press the accelerator and nothing happens, and Barry pulled up, he knew it wasn't right.'

There's a very slim chance that Sprinter might have pulled himself up, but it's not in the nature of a horse to do that. Humans and dogs will stop if they don't feel right, but a flight animal's instinct is to keep going, there's safety in numbers, so he might have tried to struggle on. 'Barry Geraghty stopped the horse, the horse didn't stop himself,' Celia emphasises. 'He's a very experienced jockey and I can only commend him. I watched the race back a number of times. As an amateur, I couldn't see what it was he felt. I suppose that's the advantage of a top-class pro like him, he's got the confidence that there's something wrong. Waiting for the horse to make up his mind wouldn't be a good idea, the horse will try to stick with the herd and the more he feels things going wrong, the more instinct is saying: keep with your friends.'

Sprinter was lucky that day; if Barry hadn't pulled him up, 'he'd have totally run out of energy,' Celia says. 'They don't usually collapse, but it's impossible that he could have carried on in any fashion we'd want to see, he'd have fallen badly behind.'

His heart corrected itself the next day, without any need for drugs or surgery. That was the good news, that he could physically recover. 'The bad news was the effect it had on him,' Celia says, 'on his confidence, his trust, his wanting to ever do that again. It's shocking for the horse, I talked with Nicky about it a lot; it's difficult not to be anthropomorphic and put human thoughts in to them, but it's not pleasant. When humans get it, they feel extremely tired, it's not painful as such but they have no energy. It's extremely off-putting and is going to make him lose his confidence.' After a bad experience on the race course, a horse might not want to try as hard the next time. 'When people say a horse is being lazy or not trying, it's much more about a lost confidence,' Celia says.

Sprinter had a long rest, Corky remembers him spending his summer days out (always in at night) and not being ridden at all, 'bringing him back very gradually, on the walker for three or four weeks, then riding at a walk and trot for months, very slow progress. Nicky would give a horse plenty of time and he still does.'

Even this half-tonne thoroughbred with a clear sense of his own magnificence and the world at his feet, could lose his self-assurance, and as he came back into light training, Nicky says his work was 'sub-par, nothing like what he used to be. He was frightened.' Celia returned to Seven Barrows, observing his on-going recovery which included heart monitors, electrocardiograms (ECG) and Bluetooth, driving alongside the horse as he exercised, watching the ECGs, making sure the rhythm was regular and the heart rate was appropriate. Seven Barrows would email the memory card files to Celia to decode them.

Celia says Nicky was 'extremely patient and he always believed in the horse too, so he was prepared to give him the time. And he chose his battles; he doesn't need to run in a lesser race to be successful, he waited until the horse was truly back and able to compete at his previous level. Everyone wanted him to be back the way he was or not at all. Nobody would want to see him hacking round in a low-grade race.'

It was painstaking stuff; Caroline Mould can't think of another trainer who would have dealt with Sprinter so well. 'He's in a league of his own. You chose the school and defer to the better knowledge. I was so fortunate.'

Corky knew he was on his way back when 'he started to preen again – look at me, upsides on the gallops, even in steady work – he was back,' and Nicky knew when he started getting stroppy. He was always housed in the quietest stable of the quietest barn, away from the hurly burly of the main square. 'Sprinter was grumpy in his box,' he says, 'he'd snarl at you. Sarwar [Mohammed, Sprinter's lad] held his head, I walked into his box every evening to feel his neck, his skin, and legs, and when I did that, he'd bite Sarwar! He knew he was well, in a good, feisty place. He got his aggression back.'

Over a year after he was pulled up, Sprinter returned to the racecourse, and was second to old foe Dodging Bullets in the Clarence House Chase at Ascot, before being pulled up in the Champion Chase at Cheltenham two months later. But then, a corner was turned, his courage caught the light, and suddenly, he was back at Cheltenham, trouncing rivals in the Shloer Chase. Now ridden by Nico de Boinville, people dared to dream. Nico remembers, 'Coming back in after the Shloer, after being out in the cold, having lost his ability, all his problems, then coming back, those were the days when the whole crowd at Cheltenham seemed to come out to welcome him back, you'll never forget those days.' The duo returned to take the Desert Orchid chase too, just to show there were no hard feelings.

Sprinter was back. Three years after his spellbinding Champion Chase, he came to reclaim his title. He didn't start as favourite and the atmosphere was nerve-shredding. When the announcer said 'three minutes to post', Nicky turned to Minty and said, 'I don't know if I'll survive this, I won't last three minutes.' For Nico, he felt the difference for this race of races but he had to detach. 'As a jockey, you have to slightly take yourself away from a lot of that, you do have to have a bit of distance from the emotion. There's no room for the emotional when you're riding, you have to be pretty cold.' In the parade ring, Nicky said to him, 'If he wants to go, let him go. Don't stop him.'

Nico remembers, 'The guv'nor always said to me "do whatever you want but do not ever disappoint this horse, go out and enjoy it. If he takes you there, he takes you there." It was my one instruction, and he used to take me there between four and three out. Coming down the hill at Cheltenham between jumping three out and two out that's where he seemed to be able to inject a bit of pace and put them to the sword.' Do not disappoint this horse: quite a brief. 'It's a fantastic instruction to have: go with him, trust him, trust your horse.'

Nicky remembers the moment when Sprinter took charge of the race, 'when he overtook Ruby, who was bowling along, thinking I'm going great, flying along, this giant black aeroplane went past him in the air and was gone! That was the end of the race in ten strides, that was the moment, probably sooner than Nico wanted, he clicked into overdrive, he changed gear, ideally it would be two fences later, but he had no option.'

Lifelong racing fan Miranda Murton was in the stands. She'd spent the entire day telling herself to stop wishing for the impossible, and remembers a certain nervous tension in the air. 'You've got to know how to handle Cheltenham or it'll overpower you,' she says. She'd tacked her way to the pre-parade rails. 'There was a gasp when he walked in,' she says, 'he was so polished, majestic, stunning. He's impossibly beautiful and handsome, and doesn't he know it! There's a real pomp about him, he's box office, a film star.'

Once the race was on, 'people were quiet initially, but the moment he came to the fourth-last and was airborne, there was a huge roar, I turned away I couldn't bear the thought of anything happening. It was a dream for us fans, then he went upsides

Un de Sceaux and Nico said come on then, what have you got, and he went past. I was crying when he was coming up the straight and I screamed when he went past the post. The roar and the noise, people were almost hysterical, the outpouring of emotion, everyone's newspapers went up, four grown men in front of me were in tears. It was astonishing. Then I ran so fast, scrambled up the step, barged through, pushing and shoving, I was rude, but I wasn't missing my horse and the welcome he got. The roof came off, it was a dream, I will never forget being there.'

Commentator Simon Holt admits to getting 'a bit emotional' but adds, 'One of the most compelling things in sport is the comeback – going back to Muhammad Ali coming back to win the world heavyweight title for the third time and Rafa Nadal for all his injuries, and in racing it's just very emotional when a horse loved by the public manages to come back and produce something like that. He wasn't expected to win, Un de Sceaux was odds-on favourite.'

He didn't prepare a script, for the simple reason that 'racing is at its core unpredictable, it's rare that it works how you think or how you want it to. Part of the job is to reflect the drama, and tell a story in a few words and not a lot of time. It's one of the great comebacks, I was very pleased with the commentary, it worked. It helps if you care. It doesn't happen very often where things work out perfectly or you get to commentate on a race people will remember for years to come.' He knew that should the impossible happen, there was a short film being prepared, scored by 'The Impossible Dream' from *Man of La Mancha*, and he thought, if it happens, I'm going to use that phrase.

'It was unbelievable when he looked to have Un de Sceaux beat coming down the hill from the second last,' he says. 'The reaction from the crowd was unbelievable, I couldn't help but get swept up in one of most memorable races I've ever had the privilege to watch. It's the emotion that goes with jump racing, memorable days, and horses so much loved.'

Nico was a lot more measured about one of the greatest comebacks of all time, 'I didn't go in with any expectations, he always felt good at home. The only time you're ever going to tell if he was back to somewhere near his best is in that last three or four furlongs. It all boiled down to the instruction: he took me there, go with him, ride the wave.' When they won, Nico hunched over his saddle, face hidden. It was unusual, a private few seconds of what? Relief? Happiness? Disbelief? 'I don't know,' Nico says, 'I couldn't even tell you, I couldn't even tell you. I know it was fantastic for him being back to winning races. We'd been through so much, from when he pulled up at Kempton, it had been such a struggle for everyone involved, so many put so much into getting him back on track – it was just an amalgamation of feelings.' And he adds, 'I don't get tearful.' His were the only dry eyes in the house, as he returned, down the chute, under the bridge, into the paddock. It was 'incredibly special'.

Nicky says of Nico's reaction, 'I think you could take it that under those circumstances, Nico and I were under some pressure. You know, it was more relief, it was job done.' It was Nicky's best day in racing and a tribute to a remarkable training performance. He gives all the credit to Sprinter, saying, 'He was brilliant. The horse did the talking.'

The only person who didn't want a ticket to Cheltenham for the 2016 Champion Chase was Celia Marr, the woman who had done so much to clear his path. She wasn't immune to his charms, 'He's such a fantastic horse, so glamorous, his presence is amazing, he looks down on the world, he's very elegant,' or to the romance of the story but she says, 'I hate going to the races, for that sort of thing. I couldn't have stood there waiting all day so I made sure I was busy.'

Her absence at Cheltenham was partly 'a luck thing; the horse either needs a vet or doesn't need a vet, and my place is when he needs a vet. The horse doesn't need his vet anymore and I don't want to hang around like a bad luck charm, it's a superstition.' Instead, she spent that week with a colleague in small animal cardiology at the University of Liverpool. She remembers, 'I snuck out from a clinic and watched the race in a coffee room. I didn't know the others there at all, they knew I was watching a horse race and knew I was very pleased with the result. After, I thought they were asking me how much the horse made so I told them the prize money (£199,325), but they thought I'd just won that on a bet!'

She says now, 'It was an astounding performance, amazing to watch. When it all panned out gloriously maybe I should have gone, but not a single person knew who I was standing in the room watching it, it was the least horse vet place I could find.'

Barry, who had left Seven Barrows by this time, says with generosity, 'There wasn't any part of me that wasn't delighted for Nicky and Nico, who deserved it. He did all the early schooling on Sprinter, he deserved the opportunity, it was brilliant for everyone.' He adds, 'Honestly, I didn't see him coming back when I left. He'd been gone nearly two years, I was at peace: we'd had our best from him but when he came back it was magic, when you saw the crowds and how much it meant to everyone.'

Minty says simply, 'It was one of the greatest feelings you could ever have in your life.' The comeback of all comebacks. Especially as he also remembers the 2016 Cheltenham preview well. 'Nicky was saying they were very hopeful they'd got him back and [retired champion jockey] Richard Johnson said, "of course you can't get a horse back".' Nicky adds, 'We'd been down to the bottom – everyone said, "Henderson, you must be joking." I dared to suggest Sprinter had a good chance in the Champion Chase and everyone said, "sentimental rubbish, he's got no chance, grow up, dry up".'

Richard Johnson OBE says now, 'It's one of the best training performances I've ever seen at that level. It's not unheard of to come back, but to lose his way and come back to win the Champion Chase, the best two-mile Champion Chase of the year? I was delighted to see it and it was great to see the atmosphere that day. I was genuinely shocked; that's one of hardest things for a trainer for lots of reasons. Even if you're lucky enough to get a good horse, to keep a good horse going at the top for season after season is an art in itself. Most horses have a good year then they can't hold it for sustained time – I would say Sprinter Sacre coming back was one of the best performances in my time riding. I'm quite happy to eat my words. Hats off! Fantastic job.'

Sprinter returned to his winning ways: at Sandown he trounced Un de Sceaux by his more traditional margin of 15 lengths and Nico said that we should be grateful for every day we get to see him on a racecourse. Then a minor tendon problem emerged and Nicky announced Sprinter's retirement in November of that year with a press conference and said we'd all have to learn to live without him. It was over. He says of that era now, 'I've never had experiences like that; pure crippling emotion. Crippling. He had us in tears – never of sorrow – and gave us days of anguish.'

Looking back on Sprinter, Caroline says, 'He was public property, that's the joy, when you see the pleasure he gave. I ended up with a horse that people dream of.' Twice, she got into a taxi, the driver saw her name and said, 'Are you that Caroline Mould?' 'Which one?' 'The owner of Sprinter Sacre?' "Yes.' 'Oh my God, that horse!' they'd say, and refuse to charge her for the ride.

'For donkey's years I've been aware of the privilege and the joy he gave so many,' she says, 'it was real theatre. You don't have the feeling of possession you might with a dog, but it's such a multi-faceted thing, you're just a part of it, it's wonderful to be in his orbit with everybody else. He loved himself, that was his appeal – horses can get away with that.'

His statistics: 18 wins, including his nine Grade Ones, his earnings of £1,136,884, don't capture the joy. 'I was very fortunate to be in the same universe. It was once in a lifetime, the pure joy he gave his adoring public – what would he have done without them? I'd watch reruns with the sound off, it was like magic to me, everything he did so beautifully, the pleasure he gave to so many. You can't be possessive about something like that, I don't need the trophy. He gave me immense pleasure, that I don't get from anything else in life,' Caroline says, still moved to tears by all that he was and all that he gave.

Everybody cried when he left the yard. Sarwar looked after Sprinter every single day, he knew him inside out. He says he would call to him when he entered his barn 'and he'd call right back'. He loved him so much, he cried more when Sprinter left than when his father died.

* * *

One day Vicky Roberts, who runs a retraining and rehabbing yard for racehorses, took a call from Nigel Twiston-Davies's assistant trainer, Carl Llewellyn.

'Can you take another horse?'

'No, I'm full to the brim, I can't fit any more in.'

'You'll like this one.'

'No, I won't.'

'It's Sprinter Sacre.'

'I'll take him.'

Years on, Vicky says he's clever, kind (happy to give her cat a ride in the field) and 'you can put any other horses in the field and he wouldn't hurt them', though that may be because they instinctively know he's the boss and he's not taking questions at this time.

'When I take their breakfast out, if someone else gets to the feed first, as soon as he starts walking towards them, they move out of his way, but he's also very needy. If he's down at the bottom of the field grazing and the other two walk off to the top, he starts screaming and shouting and galloping to the top, he can't be on his own.'

Vicky used to be a conditional flat jockey, and once in a huge field, Sprinter was messing around and she said to him, oh, go on then, do what you want. 'We went from zero to 60 in one second flat. The size of the horse, the speed and power, he's a freak. He's as fast as a six-furlong sprinter but he can keep it up for two miles.'

She adds, 'He's a funny horse, I was having a conversation with him the other day out riding, it's probably taken him till this year to fully trust me and be completely dependent and reliant on me. He trusts me implicitly and I trust him with my life now but it's taken him a long time. He had such a strong relationship in training with Sarwar.'

He still needs an audience, still bites, still knows his best angles for a photograph, is still unfazed by his effect – instant tears – on his fans, still canters on the spot, bucks all the way home, now 'slams his feet on the floor: I'm retired, I don't have to go out in the rain!'

When hacking in company he 'has to have his head in front' or he will bite the other horses, and he still parades. At Seven Barrows, for Open Days, he stands on the lawn, right by the sign that says 'please keep off the grass' and he still draws awed crowds wherever he goes. The first time Vicky took him back to parade at Cheltenham, she said to her assistant Lucy, 'Don't talk to me, don't look at anyone, just look at the ground, because it's going to be so emotional,' and as soon as they started walking they both burst into tears. His price will always be a mystery, but his worth is clear to see.

11

ALTIOR

The spine-tingling star with a swagger and 19 straight victories

NICKY'S BUSINESS cards are too big for a wallet, and they don't carry any of his details. In fact, they're a stack of two glossy A4 photos. One is of a horse at full stretch, with a leap that was later measured at 14 yards, about the length of a double decker bus – 'that's Altior's card' – and the other photo is of Sprinter Sacre. 'I just keep them in my bag because you get in a taxi or you see somebody and they say are you this or that, and you scribble his name on the back.'

The huge, record-setting life that Altior lived started small. His dam, Monte Solaro, was the first horse that Paddy Behan (senior) ever owned and his son Paddy (junior, quoted here) helped him pick pedigrees and now they do this together but 'dad's the man that bred him' and he took a liking to the sire High Chaparral.

'We were always just trying to put speed into the horse,' Paddy says. 'It's not easy looking at a horse running three-and-a-half miles around bottomless ground, because it's hard on them, but to watch Altior's turn of speed, there's something exciting about it.'

Altior was only with them for a few months, but 'he was always very racy-looking,' Paddy says. 'We were new to it, we know how to look after them very well, we know real good from real bad but not in between; we've got better.' The mini Altior had 'a bit of fire' in him but 'you could always manage him; his full brother was very tricky and Altior wasn't tricky, he loved to mess around and act the bollocks, as we say in Ireland'. The family bred two foals a year, and never more than that so they were looked after with one-on-one treatment all the time and Altior was just their fourth. 'To land a horse like that is special,' Paddy says, though now they're consumed with how to direct lightning to the same spot.

When Mick and Ciara Carty from Kilmoney Cottage Stud arrived at the yard, Paddy remembers, 'They said "the way your foal strides is unbelievable, that's as good a horse as you'll ever see". You never know if it'll materialise, and we sold him from the field.' He adds wistfully, 'I'd love to be leading him in and out every day at home, I didn't get to spend much time with him.'

A foal's life moves fast; up on their feet within an hour, nursing within two, the mare should pass the placenta in three, and weaning from four months. Altior was a May foal, bought by Ciara and her husband in the September, and she remembers her first impressions of him. 'He was a beautiful foal, very athletic, and that's all you go on. He had great presence about him, all quality, lovely conformation, and a super mover; he took off across the field and he wouldn't break eggs under his feet.' In the yard he was 'boisterous, a great character, he'd catch your eye, playful, always saying look at me; a show off'. After an 8am Sunday morning negotiation, with whiskey, he was theirs.

There must have been something special in their turf, because the Cartys reared him with the horse that would go on to be Minella Rocco, the two winning at Cheltenham in the same year and Ciara says, 'We probably didn't expect him to grow so big. He was so young when we bought him, his mum wasn't a big mare, but every year he developed into a beautiful-looking horse, and by the time he got to three, in frame and temperament he was very straightforward, always wanted to please you in his work, so easy-going, always in your hand, forward-going, happy doing his work, very light on his feet, intelligent, gorgeous, everything came easily to him.'

The Cartys took their beautiful three-year-old with the perfect white diamond star and one white sock to the Goffs sale and capsized everyone. Ciara had a job to match his walking pace, but she'd never, ever do anything to hold a racehorse back: 'You only interfere with them if you pull them back.' She knows Minty of old and says 'he knows what he's looking for, he's years at it, and while Altior's pedigree was probably more for the flat, he was sharp and full of quality'.

Minty appeared, said, 'Well!' and brought Nicky. Ciara remembers, Nicky 'stood into him, said "Wow", and stood back and just watched him, he didn't look at him for long, he knows what he wants and he did everything he likes. He's a great, outstanding judge. It's something you have or you haven't. Minty has it and Nicky has the training, it's not something you can learn so much from other people, but you have to have something that gives you that feeling when you see a horse, you know it's a racehorse. Not everyone has it but some seem to buy more of the better horses than others. They say it's your eye, a good eye for a horse. Some don't look at pedigree at all, it's the individual horse.'

Minty and Nicky knew at once. 'I fell in love with him as soon as I saw him,' Nicky says, 'I said to Minty, "we're getting him". He was – and is – a good-looking horse, very athletic with a good walk and lot of presence.' Minty says the Derby-winning High Chaparral wasn't a 'classic jumping sire' but Altior 'had a bit of class in his pedigree and a pretty good jumping mare'. High Chaparral was sired by Sadler's Wells, who was sired by Northern Dancer. Big names. The sire is so important for Minty; there are some he won't have, and while some sterling individuals come with a 'ropey pedigree', he will take a chance on a horse if the right sire's on his list. Altior swapped hands for €60,000, a stupendous bargain in hindsight for a horse that went on to earn over £1.32 million, (though no one buys a racehorse with a view to making their money back. It's not that kind of investment; no one needs to be warned that your investment may go down as well as up and you may get back less blah blah).

'We were educating him from the very beginning,' Nicky says. He was just one of a group of unknown three-year-olds that arrived as raw material like a slab of marble in the hands of a skilled sculptor and Nicky didn't have to wait too long to see something start to take shape. 'The cream rises to the top very quickly,' he says. How quickly? 'As soon as they started to do some work,' he says. 'As soon as you turned him in to face the first fence, he was gone, he loved it.'

Stable lad Aaron Rid remembers watching Altior schooling and 'it would make the hair on your neck stand up. He'd give you a different feeling, rubbing along, coming up from nowhere, not in a dangerous way, he knew where his feet were, he was wicked clever.' Nico de Boinville, first on his back, says, 'He was very precocious, intelligent and he had size and scope. He attacked the fences, and I was thinking, wow, we've got something special here.'

Altior didn't grace the turf till the back end of the season, at Market Rasen in a bumper and he was 'one of the biggest certainties that ever walked out of this yard,' Nicky says. He went off as favourite and won by 14 lengths, and 'he'd never run before, odds on, the whole place would have been mortified let alone broke if he'd got beaten. It wasn't possible unless we'd got it so wrong. We thought he was a superstar.'

It all started in earnest at Chepstow, on 10 October 2015 in the Novices' Hurdle for what Nicky calls the first serious day of the season, 'We knew what we'd got, he jumped for fun, he was never off the bridle and he won by 34 lengths. Then it all started, that's how he got to 19 consecutive wins, and that was number one.'

He picked off all-comers in his novice hurdling starts at Ascot, Cheltenham and Kempton. Commentator Simon Holt remembers, 'He was expected to win, from his Novices' Hurdle at Kempton on Boxing Day on, which was the sort of occasion where press men say, "that's a good horse". He swept to victory; it was astonishing. It was the same when Kauto Star made his debut at Newbury. There's a manner of victory, you know it, it hits you in the face when you see something special.'

Altior arrived at the Festival for the Supreme Novices' Hurdle and despite the Willie Mullins army appearing over the horizon, Nicky remembers, 'I really didn't think there was a horse that could beat him, it turned out to be true.' The favourite Min (who went on to win seven Grade Ones), was second by seven lengths and Buveur d'Air (who would go on to win two Champion Hurdles) was third. These horses were more than worthy competitors and Altior's jockey, Nico, says he'll never forget it, 'The calibre of the race, it was a who's who of the last generation of horses that have all gone on to be superstars in their own right.'

It was his fifth consecutive win and it started the age of Altior: he'd arrived. Paddy remembers watching the race abroad, and 'nobody knew how good he was, I presume Nicky knew, but we didn't know and to see him come over that last hurdle and blitz Min, an unbelievable horse, still, even now I remember. My brother has a recording of Dad; seeing him leave the chair and leave the ground was a sight to behold.' Whenever Altior ran, Paddy senior would collect his old mama, Monte, from the field, and say softly to her, 'You did it again, Monte, you did it again.'

Miranda Murton fell for Altior the moment he graced the parade ring. She says, 'He had an aura, he wasn't flashy, but he really had presence, he was noble, stunning, with the most beautiful head, kind eyes, beautifully turned out, as Nicky's horses always are.' After the Supreme, she remembers, 'it was so exciting, the roar from the crowd, and seeing a young beautiful horse coming up the straight. I couldn't believe Nicky had got another superstar, he made it all look so easy.' She remembers being in the Arkle bar at Cheltenham and 'a complete stranger said, "make the most of him, you won't see one like that for a long time". I'm lucky I've seen him light up racecourses, and the ovations he received.'

Paddy Jnr visited Altior at Seven Barrows, and remembers, 'Nicky was so courteous, he took us in to the kitchen for the morning meeting with the jockeys, having breakfast, then tipping up the hill in the car showing us the works. He told us, "Altior is an amazing animal, a freak, he's the best."' Paddy Snr never went to watch Altior racing; instead he sat in the same chair, with his wife in the same place, watching his second-best television, for every single race and 'you wouldn't be able to say anything to him the day of the race because he'd snap at you,' says his son.

At the end of 2016, Altior routed Black Corton in the Novices' Chase at Kempton by 63 lengths (in the two-horse race, the horse was still coming up to the last as Altior was past the post), and everywhere he went – Kempton, Sandown, Newbury and Cheltenham on a loop – he left his top-flight competitors in his wake. The pressure on Nicky to keep it coming was immense; everyone assumed Altior would win, and only other-worldly perfection would do. It helped that he had what Nicky describes as 'the will to be good, he wanted to win and please and he was a joy to train, and jumping so good it scared me. He knew he was good-looking, with a great swagger.' Minty always says the temperament is the thing and Altior had good nature to spare. He was a darling, but no pushover, he 'had some sass, he'd put up a little argument with you', says Aaron Rid, who looked after Altior in his later years. But then, 'you'd take a picture of his face over the stable door and he didn't even look real, he looked like a painting'.

Nicky didn't give Nico many instructions in the parade ring, they knew what there was to know, and when it was just the three of them, for a few private seconds, his final advice was to go and enjoy himself, have fun. Nico says, 'That reassurance and support is crucial to give you the flexibility to do what you need to do on the track.' It looked so easy, but Nico says, 'You never have an easy race in Grade Ones because you're up against the best. Ultimately these champions, from the final fence or hurdle to the line is where they do their best bit of work and put distance between themselves and the rest of the field. These champion two-milers, they've got something about them. He could be fresh as you like, but in the paddock at Sandown, full of people, immediately he'd start switching on and strutting his stuff. Sprinter the same – they know when the public's watching them and when the cameras are on, they put their best foot forward.'

When Nico says it's all about what happens after the last, it's true, but what we see as a final burst of speed can be an optical illusion. Associate Professor Dr Jane Williams from Hartpury University notes that quite often the speed of the second half of a race is slightly increased from the first half, but in the final furlongs they're usually slowing down, not speeding up. 'It's that visual trick, isn't it?' she says. 'Because they look like they're flat out, and everything's going, and, everyone's driving, it looks like they're getting faster, but actually it's about maintaining as much speed as you can at the end.'

It was where Altior always did his best work. He kept something back, ready to produce it like a bunch of flowers from a magician's sleeve, just at the right time and he evolved through his career, learning how to conserve his energy. Nico says, 'When he was very young, he was very gassy, sharp, and on it all the time and most of the time it was just about trying to calm him down. As he got older, he became very relaxed and laid back then it was just trying to galvanise him through the period of being relaxed, then he found his extra kick.'

In 2017, his tenth straight win came at the Festival, in the Grade One Arkle, when he saw off Cloudy Dream by six lengths, just after he saw off old pros like Fox Norton by 13 lengths and Dodging Bullets a further five lengths behind in the Game Spirit Chase at Newbury, and just before he trounced seriously good Special Tiara by eight lengths in the Grade One Celebration Chase at Sandown, surging clear after the second last. Nicky told reporters his plan for the 2018/19 season was Sandown for the Tingle Creek, Ascot for the Clarence House, then Cheltenham for the Champion Chase. It was all Altior's for the taking and it all came to pass.

Nicky's highlights were the two Champion Chases, because 'they are the pinnacle, he was playing in top company at the top level every time'. In the first, the combined forces of Min and Paul Townend, Politologue and Sam Twiston-Davies, Douvan, Special Tiara and Charbel – all household names, sterling chasers – were unable to get any closer than seven lengths to him and in 2019, Politologue and Harry Cobden, Sceau Royal and Daryl Jacob, Min and Ruby Walsh, Ordinary World and Rachael Blackmore, again had to make do with what was left. His second Champion Chase wasn't perfect, he showed he was flesh and blood after all, when he made a mistake at the water jump and had to show his mettle up the hill to equal the 18 consecutive wins of Big Buck's (over hurdles, Altior's tally included fences).

The commentator Simon Holt remembers it well, 'When he won the second Champion Chase, he didn't look like winning, and he was incredible from the final fence. All through his career he was unstoppable from the last, pulling it out of the fire. It was getting harder, and he looked like he wanted a bit further, maybe he'd lost a yard of speed.' Miranda recalls: 'He came from quite far back, he fought like a lion coming up the hill, you knew he'd stay, he suddenly flew the last one. Nico timed it so well, he had great stamina coming up the hill, it played to his strengths.' Looking back now, she says, 'He was joyful, he spent so much time in the air, he was a wonderful jumper, so classy, poetry in motion, he tugged at your heart strings. He was majestic, and I followed him everywhere.'

In between those two Chases came the 2018 Tingle Creek in torrential rain where Nico remembers feeling the rain dripping down the inside of his back pad. He says, 'It became a match race with Altior and Un de Sceaux and, when Ruby was in the plate, there was no quarter given, so that was special.' Ruby Walsh set a furious pace on soft ground, Altior's white breast girth was camouflaged entirely by mud, Nico's colours and Altior's perfect white diamond were barely visible. It wasn't the ground that would suit a sudden change of gear. Ruby had dictated the terms of the race, but when Nico made his move to the last, Altior leapt to answer the call.

He was revered wherever he went. Raising the roof and breaking records, cheered back to the winner's enclosure, though for Nico, the winning feeling is momentary: 'As soon as you've done it and crossed the line, the feeling is never quite the same, a moment of elation and then it's gone and you're on to the next one.' AP says the feeling lasts until you take the silks off. 'I'd say it's even sooner than that,' Nico responds.

Altior's record-setting 19th straight win was back at Sandown for the Celebration Chase, pushing Sceau Royal into second. From 10 October 2015 to 27 April 2019, Altior lit up the turf. Simon Holt says, 'He ran up a long sequence of wins, always odds-on and people admired the horse. It's only when they have to battle and it doesn't seem so easy, can it bring a lump to the throat.'

He can only be talking about November 2019, Ascot, Cyrname and the Christy 1965 Grade Two Chase. The public and the press can get at Nicky when they think he's being soft and not running his horses, because the ground's not right, and because all he thinks about is Cheltenham, Cheltenham, Cheltenham – and that rankles him. Altior was adored by his public; he was a record-breaking superstar, a thriller, and they wanted to see him, at the pinnacle of his career. This is the background.

Nicky says, 'I made one howling mistake, running him first time out over two-and-a-half miles. He'd never been that far before. It rained and rained and it was bottomless and Cyrname went off at a million miles an hour and beat us. Fine. Paul [Nicholls] had got him incredibly fit and we weren't incredibly fit, we were ready for our first run. Running over that distance first time was absolutely stark raving bonkers.'

He'd discussed it with Altior's owners, Pat and Christopher Pugh who were abroad, 'after a sleepless night and um-ing and ah-ing, it was his prep, there was nowhere else to go, we felt we had to go for it. Soft ground can be much harder work for some than others.

'The Pughs always went with whatever I decided. They understood, there was lots of discussion, they were always very keen we stayed at two miles. Then it became obvious he'd benefit from further, which was why we moved up. I've regretted it ever since. There were only three runners and we paid the penalty; I wouldn't have run him that day, the third horse was not a contender and there was a big build-up to the clash with them. I should have taken him out that morning and I didn't because of the public, and the horse paid the penalty. It would have been a lot better over two miles, Paul's horse was always going to go flat out; he had trained him for the race and I'd probably underdone it. He hadn't had a racecourse gallop, Paul had, he played the game better if you like, he got his horse very, very fit.'

It pains him, still. 'I ran him, because of the public, he struggled, they ruined each other and never recovered. The two vets that followed him in said he was almost unconscious and Nico couldn't ride him to the unsaddling post. He was like a boxer in the ring that has been flattened. He was alright an hour later, but it's not the right way to do it, it was the beginning of the end, and I did it because I couldn't face taking him out and ruining the whole day for everybody. I knew the flack that would happen. I couldn't do it to Ascot, the public, television, the whole world was sitting on it. Everyone wants to see horses like that running against each other every week but it can't happen. A horse of Altior's quality has only a handful of races to choose from every year.'

Nicky says now that he got to the bottom of Altior that day, 'and you shouldn't do that to a horse. You've gone too deep, the scars are there laid to bear, they don't recover mentally or physically, you dug too deep. Horses like that are that good, they will gallop till they drop. The bravest was Bobs Worth, he didn't know when to give up, he'd go beyond the call of duty. Neither Paul nor I should have taken each other on the first time out, beginning of the season, that was wrong as a prep race for their first run of the year.'

Nico remembers it well. 'The guv'nor and I were in the paddock looking at Altior, and Cyrname, and there wasn't a scrap of condition on Cyrname, he was as fit as a horse can be. We were probably not, we weren't ready. We were ready to have a run but not a dust-up as it turned out to be. I slightly knew, and I tried to be as easy as I could be on him, without disappointing everyone but I knew coming up the hill it wasn't going to be happening today.' He needed his extra kick and it wasn't there. He says now, 'You have to give it a go, and we did, at the same time I wasn't overly hard on him. That's my job as well, when it's not happening to save your horse for another day and I did that to the best of my ability and it wasn't to be. I felt he was very tired and the ground was fairly soft,' and it was, he adds 'one of those nightmare days that you won't forget.'

Miranda remembers Nico walking Altior back, 'The horse looked so forlorn, he'd given everything, I was in tears like a lot of people, I was so worried about him, and everyone was clapping and saying, "We still love you Altior."'

Simon Knapp is the veterinary advisor to the racecourse association, and senior racecourse veterinary surgeon. He was in charge at Ascot that day. Nico dismounted to lead him back and Simon recalls it clearly. 'There was a general hush and surprise at the time; most people gather round the winners, not the unsaddling enclosure. There was a sense that something had happened.' He goes on, 'In my career there are few horses I've seen as tired as that horse when he finished. He was absolutely exhausted. They took each other on, I don't think either were in a great state when they finished but Altior was worse of the two. He was out of his feet, totally exhausted as he walked off the course.'

He and his colleagues were all taken aback by the race, that they took each other on as strongly as they did, on ground that was

One eye on the camera; Sprinter Sacre with Barry Geraghty before the Champion Chase, Punchestown, 2013. 'I expect Sprinter knows he became an idol,' says his owner Caroline Mould.

Taking flight, Punchestown, 2013. 'He could make three lengths in the air, he could jump himself from fifth to first in a flash then he'd be set alight,' Barry Geraghty remembers.

A horseman and his horse. Nicky with Sprinter Sacre, Newbury, 2014.

The dream comes true as Sprinter Sacre re-takes the Queen Mother Champion Chase with Nico de Boinville, Cheltenham Festival, 2016.

Nico is led back to the winner's enclosure. 'We'd been through so much,' he says. 'It had been such a struggle for everyone involved, so many put so much into getting him back on track.'

Nicky holds an emotional press conference at Cheltenham, November 2016, to announce Sprinter Sacre's retirement. 'We're going to miss him,' he said. 'It's been a great journey … life will have to go on without him.'

Sprinter Sacre still parades for his adoring public, and is seen here with Vicky Roberts, at the Seven Barrows Open Day. The rules around keeping off the grass do not apply.

Perfection: Sprinter Sacre with his lad, Sarwar Mohammed at Seven Barrows, 2016.

He's a diamond: Altior after winning the Clarence House Chase, Ascot, 2019.

One of Altior's leaps was measured at 14 yards, about the same length as a double decker bus. Seen here with Noel Fehily, taking the Novices' Chase, Sandown 2016.

Altior and Nico de Boinville on their way to winning the Tingle Creek, Sandown 2018. 'It became a match race with Altior and Un de Sceaux ... there was no quarter given, so that was special,' he remembers.

Nicky takes in Altior, after his Game Spirit Chase, Newbury, 2017.

Seeing things the same way: Altior with his groom Mohammed Hussein at the 2017 Seven Barrows Owners' Day.

The Christy 1965 Chase, Ascot 2019. Nico dismounts before leading an exhausted Altior to the unsaddling area, having been beaten by Cyrname in an unforgiving race that brought an end to his 19 straight wins. 'I've regretted it ever since,' says Nicky. 'He was like a boxer in the ring that's been flattened.'

Debbie Matthews meets her hero Altior for the first time at Seven Barrows, 2019. She says, 'I have so much to thank him for, there will never be another. He saved me.'

Might Bite sails over the water jump in the RSA Chase at the 2017 Festival, giving no indication that after the last he will make a sharp right-hand turn towards the stables, before re-joining the race at the last minute and claiming victory.

Might Bite and Nico de Boinville head to head with eventual winners Native River and Richard Johnson in the 2018 Gold Cup. 'I could have been beaten 20 lengths,' Nico says. 'My memory tells me I got beaten a long, long way because I was so deflated.'

Barry Geraghty's then nine-year-old daughter, Órla, leads the three-year-old Constitution Hill home. Barry says, 'He wasn't completely docile and dopey, but he had good energy, he was good fun, in a playful way, and a really kind individual.' [Barry Geraghty]

Constitution Hill interrupts his holiday to catch up with Nicky, 2023.

Inch perfect: Constitution Hill and Nico de Boinville clear the last on the way to winning the Champion Hurdle, Cheltenham, 2023.

Corky checked every horse's leg, every single morning; he's a Lambourn legend.

Talking the same language: Corky at Seven Barrows, 2004.

Nicky watches his team warming up in the covered school, 2010. He says, 'I ask every single rider every single morning, "All OK? All happy?" before we set off and when they come back. Knowing your horses is the most important thing.'

Nicky watches Altior on the gallops, ridden by Aaron Rid in 2021. Altior had 'the will to be good', Nicky says. 'He wanted to win and please and he was a joy to train, and jumping so good it scared me. He knew he was good-looking, with a great swagger.'

Nicky receives the OBE for services to racing in the New Year's Honours list 2020 with his daughters, from left Tessa, wife Sophie, Sarah and Camilla.

'taxing' at best, and they had an uneasy feeling that it wasn't going to end well. It was worse than they thought, when they saw Altior 'dead on his feet, out for the count, we weren't expecting that. We'd been expecting two tired horses, and the degree of exhaustion of both of them, especially Altior, was beyond the norm by a very long way.'

The treatment for him at the time was controlled walking and cold water; all the scientific breakthroughs have yet to come up with anything better. Walking quietly allows the horse to disperse the blood supply through his muscles as all the lactic acid that has built up needs to disperse, and horses get very hot when they're that tired. This was the acute phase, to get over the exhaustion, and he walked back to the stables. 'You're always fearful they could collapse,' Simon says. 'He had his heart checked, that's why everything is there ready to go. If he deteriorated, he would have had all sorts of medical intervention, but we try not to because we don't want to mask anything going forward.'

While Simon says that horses can recover from that degree of exhaustion, there's a physical element, there is lasting damage, probably muscular. He remembers a horse at Royal Ascot that got loose and did three circuits: 'Every time he passed the crowd, they cheered and he went round again. He wasn't lame, but he left everything on the track, he was never the same and he never raced again.'

Simon with his years of experience and expertise has nothing but compassion for the position Nicky was in, and in all his time dealing with horses on the racecourse, he sees him as 'probably the most astute trainer I know, with a very high regard for his horses. These are top-quality horses and because of that, they're brave, they aren't wimps, for want of a better word, they are brave and will push themselves to the limit. That's the difference between the top and moderate athletes, who will go the extra distance.'

There's a saying that moderate horses never hurt themselves because they don't push themselves beyond their limit, and the exceptional will lay themselves on the line, and there are consequences. Simon Knapp says, 'We talk about remarkable horses but if you look at Nicky's record, he's a remarkable trainer. He knows exactly which horse is where, he always finds a good stamp of horse – good-looking and beautifully turned out – he always has them ready, gets them fit, gets them jumping well, knows where to place them, has a good team around, good jockeys, it's a very professional enterprise.'

It was a dire experience, but Simon places no blame at Nicky's door. Having observed him at close range for many years, he thinks 'it's not even a regard, it's a deep love for horses, he's a horseman with a deep love for horses and there's a difference. It's part of how astute and brilliant [he is] and part of his success is understanding and love of the horse. I think they are within the fabric of his make-up, in his psyche, he's got horses in his blood.'

Corky says Altior was the supreme horse, the champion of champions, and better than Sprinter ('19 out of 19! Come on!'). He was hard to keep sound, with little problems here and there and always an absolute gentleman. After Ascot, Corky remembers telling Nicky it was 'the first time he'd made a mistake, and he knew, and he should have put his foot down'. When Altior came off the lorry, Corky was distressed by what he saw. 'It was terrible, he came off like a tired horse. It's terrible to see a horse stressed, he was dead in himself, no life, no interest, nothing. It was devastating. I took him out next day for a pick of grass, normally when you lead him, he's jumping and kicking; he had his head down, no life in him.'

Nico says he was never the same horse again, though he did win once more at Newbury in his next race, beating Sceau Royal into second again. At home, he worked brilliantly, and showed a glimpse of his old spark; he recovered. He adds, 'The boss is a lot harder on himself for that race than he should be because ultimately it was a race, and we all gave it a good go.'

Nicky's never let himself be talked into a race again. He still takes nothing more sophisticated than a wooden 'going stick' with him when he walks a course with his jockey to see how deep into the earth it goes, to see if the ground is too hard or soft. It's not an exact science but if he doesn't like what he sees, he's not running his horses.

* * *

Debbie Matthews wasn't a racing fan but when she was pregnant and sofa-bound, she found herself half-heartedly watching the Festival to keep her daughter company. 'I had no clue who he was,' she says, of the moment she saw Altior, 'but I thought, that horse looks like he's flying, and he won the race. When they led him in, I saw the perfect diamond, I thought, what a beautiful horse, and I realised it was Altior.' She'd just witnessed his six-length win in the Arkle.

Something surprising was lit, immediately. The horse had sent her a sign. She used him as a focus to get through a difficult pregnancy and other issues that followed. She told herself that Altior would one day be the reason she got out of the house and the increasingly small life she'd boxed herself into.

That day was the Clarence House Chase at Ascot in January 2019. She tweeted that she was going to face-down her social anxiety, go to Ascot, see Altior. She received so many messages while she was driving there, she thought her children were in danger. 'I almost couldn't believe I was there, it was an awful January day, freezing, misty, and I watched him on the big screen.'

She says now, 'As a teenager I never had a thing for pop-stars but it was a bit like seeing your hero.'

The next week she was invited to Seven Barrows to meet Altior. She had never been around racehorses, and imagined they were permanently highly strung and an entirely overwhelming presence and that she wouldn't be able to get anywhere near him. She didn't know Altior; he stood next to her, quiet and still.

He was always thus. On his summer holidays with the Vigorses Tracy says, he was naturally well-mannered, 'happy to share his food, loving scratching with other horses', and often found pestering the late, great Bobs Worth. 'He's very kind,' Tracy says, 'he enjoys being groomed and cuddled, and he knows when to switch gears.' One of her favourite sights was watching him being turned out with nine other horses for the first time: shoes off, rolling, bucking, being a horse.

When Debbie stood with Altior, 'it was surreal,' she says, 'and at the same time I felt a huge sense of personal achievement, and incredibly lucky'. She'd imagined that his racecourse persona would fill all the space, as an uncontained force of nature, but his private side was gentle, curious, knowing. She says, 'I would never have understood the calming presence they have, by being next to them, looking into their eye and having a hand on them.'

Debbie went to Altior's every race, and set up an initiative to take others who suffer from anxieties to the races or to yards to see the horses in the flesh. He was the catalyst. 'He enabled me to live and not just exist,' she says now. 'I was just getting through every day and now I'm living my best life. I have so much to thank him for, there will never be another. He saved me.'

Equine therapy is as old as time. Hippocrates, the ancient Greek physician and founding father of modern medicine, wrote about 'riding's healing rhythm'. A research project by Hartpury University in conjunction with Sirona Therapeutic Horsemanship in 2020 looked at the impact of equine assisted therapy for young people (aged 6-19) most at risk of developing mental health issues over a 12-week programme. The participants interacted with the horses, learned about horse behaviour, horsemanship and communication skills, and their pre- and post-assessment wellbeing score improved by nearly 70 per cent in confidence, calmness, communication, resilience and positivity.

* * *

At age 11, Altior's owners, the Pughs decided that their 'once-in-a-generation horse' should retire. He had won 21 of his 26 starts including ten Grade Ones, four Festival wins and at his peak was the highest rated horse in training. Their statement paid tribute to Seven Barrows team, the 'genius' Nicky and 'all the wonderful racegoers who have supported Altior throughout his career'.

Nicky admits, 'At the time I begged them to go on, he was 11 rising 12 and in hindsight they were probably right. His last run at Sandown, though he was beaten, showed us he'd still got it and was coming back. He was due to have a summer out and we talked about it a lot – I did anyway.'

He's now retired to be part of Mick Fitzgerald's family. Mick sees himself as his caretaker. He no longer rides, after breaking his neck in a fall, but his wife does. In early 2023, Altior suffered a terrible, life-threatening bout of colic. He had two operations, including a four-hour surgery. His owner Pat Pugh barely left his side, Nicky and Mick visited, and the vets kept a round-the-clock vigil. Miranda admits to ringing the surgery, 'I said, 'I'm really sorry, I don't want to bother you, I'm terribly worried about Altior. I don't own him but he's my favourite, will you give him a cuddle from me?' The nurse said, "Of course I will."' Altior recovered, he's as tough as the diamond on his perfect face. He lives on.

12

MIGHT BITE

The sensitive beauty, by turns eccentric and unbeatable

MIGHT BITE liked things to be just so and early in his career at Seven Barrows, he gave his lad, Aaron Rid, an idea of the standards he expected. 'We were coming down the gallop and the tail string on his exercise sheet went up his back end,' he remembers. 'Being a young lad, I was a bit lackadaisical and the string had come undone. It was a windy day, I was trying to grab it, the sheet was flapping everywhere, and as I was trying to hold on to it, he bucked me off. He just decided to bury me, and run off across the ploughed field. I was in the Jeep trying to catch him as he was running about.'

Nicky says the same about Might Bite's strong sense of self: 'He was a lovely horse, and you couldn't bully him. He needed treating with kid gloves the whole time, we did what he wanted to do and we didn't make him do anything he didn't want to. He was so beautiful, too good-looking for his own good. Soft as butter. He was a bit too pretty, not precious – or he was a bit – he got precious.'

Beauty confers an absolute power, and as Aaron says, 'He was stunning looking, dark, dark bay, flashy looking, and he knew he was a good-looking chap, he was full of himself.' Even when a youngster, 'it took him a long time to come to hand. He was a shell for a long time, big, leggy, athletic and he took a long time to fill out. No one really had their heart set on him. He'd try and kick everything and everyone, he'd nip and bite and he had me off once or twice. He was a bit of a rogue.' Hence the name, in part. He was a 'completely different character, a freak in his own right. He had a lot of his sire, Scorpion, in him,' Nicky says, and if he's in the pedigree, the chances are his offspring is going to bite. Nicky's named the sister from the same dam, Knotted Midge, and sired by Milan, Love Bite.

Might Bite was Scorpion's most successful offspring, by the number of wins (tied at ten with Play the Ace), and earnings (over £606,915) and ratings. He was the one. As Minty says, with 40-odd years of specialist experience, the sire's temperament is hugely important, because 'lots of fidgety, excitable or exuberant horses go to stud and it's amazing how it transmits through into their progeny. It runs through stallion lines. The ideal temperament is someone who couldn't give a stuff about anything, he gets on with life, doesn't get too excited about things.' He knew Scorpion of old, and his offspring were renowned for their 'character; some were pretty fiery, not very nice, not very genuine', though no one's saying that about Might Bite, who was sent to Nicky by the groom at JP McManus's Martinstown stud.

Nicky knew enough about him to know that he had an engine but he wasn't brilliant at home, he was quite ordinary (this is a positive; performers are often entirely unremarkable when they're not 'on', so too horses). 'You love the horses that don't do it at home and really put their head down in the afternoon,' Nicky explains. 'The hardest horses to fathom and love are brilliant in the morning and not as good as they tell you in the afternoon, they're not up for the fight, and they could gallop over everything.'

Minty was sitting round the kitchen table with Nicky, and remembers, 'He said, "He's quite good, you'd better have a share," so I did. It was pure luck.' The horse turned Nicky's younger sister

Josie's head, too. She says, 'We were having a drink on the Good Friday open day and he was mentioned,' she says. 'I pricked up my ears, and Patrick Harty took us out and showed us. Patrick was very tall, Might Bite was very tall, the two were a wonderful pair. Might Bite looked so gorgeous.' Spontaneously she joined the syndicate of ten and they all became firm friends. 'I don't think anyone had any expectations, you hope, but you never think it'll be it.'

Hurdling was just a brisk warm-up; he was so impressive, Nicky decided to take him for his fences debut to the Novices' Chase at Cheltenham in November 2015. He thought he'd fly, but the horse didn't like it and decided not. Nicky says, 'Now I know Cheltenham is not a good idea for a first time, because they're big solid fences and they take a bit of jumping. Might Bite ballooned the first, he went to the moon, lost ten lengths and the second the same, after four fences he was 100 yards behind and he was meant to win!' Aaron describes his early jumping style as 'looking like a pool table thrown over a wall'.

'I frightened the living daylights out of him,' Nicky says now, 'by running him over fences first time ever at Cheltenham. It's a bigger track than most. They're big fences. And he blew them. He had to give up after four fences, he couldn't jump them. So, we had to put him back over hurdles for a whole year, and then got him built up in confidence again and then started again. And he became a great horse, but his first run over fences he couldn't jump at all. He was absolutely petrified. He was pretty wet, to be honest with you. But he was good. We loved him.'

Once he'd grown into his long legs, and had a win over hurdles, he tried the fences again for the Novices' Chase at Ffos Las. He went off as favourite but he wasn't quite right, not completely fluent and he stumbled at the last, and was beaten four lengths by Binge Drinker. Nico de Boinville says of his erstwhile partner, 'He wasn't straightforward, but he could do anything. He got beat on his first novice chase at Ffos Las which didn't go down very well but after that he never put a foot wrong – until he did what he did in the RSA chase which I don't think I've ever seen a horse do.' Being beaten that first time out was about the only time Nicky gave Nico 'a bit of a bollocking: what are you doing, ballooning everything?'

Before the RSA, though, Might Bite had coasted home by 14 lengths at Doncaster with Daryl Jacob and then lined up for the Kauto Star Novices' Chase at Kempton again with Daryl. The entire field watched him disappear into the distance from four out and he was 18 lengths clear at the last, cruising for an effortless-looking win. As Nicky remembers, he 'only had to pop over, he'd got half an hour, it was already won', and Daryl gave him a smack with his whip, and he turned an alarming somersault over the last.

Josie says, 'It wasn't his fault, he only fell once, and he was so far in front, when Daryl gave him a reminder, it threw him. He was a very intelligent horse, very bright, always interested in everything, very conscious of himself, he knew what he could do.' He was unscathed from the Catherine wheel fall, and to prove it, he won the Novices' Chase at Doncaster by 30 lengths, again drawing well clear of the field and still on the bit from six out. Josie felt 'positively sick, he was going round jumping by himself, so far ahead of everyone, I could hardly watch, it was so nerve-wracking'.

Might Bite had shown everyone what he could do. He returned to Cheltenham for the RSA Chase, and Nico gave him a 'come on then' smack with the whip. This time, he didn't fall, but he did make a sharp right-hand turn after the last. Nico remembers, 'I was thinking, what are you doing? I know what you're doing, you're trying to go home, get back to the paddock. Luckily, he saw a loose horse and he took off again. As a jockey you're such a small bit of weight on their back compared to what they are, you're effectively nothing, and if they don't want to go, they won't go, they don't have to listen to you. Luckily, when he did decide to go his tremendous turn of foot got us all out of trouble. I can't think what the embarrassment would have been if he'd got beaten.'

Minty says the handbrake turn showed the horse's character and 'how he came back was even more astonishing. That's probably where the Scorpion tendency came out, he gave a lot of his progeny that reputation, and one step further back, Montjeu, sire of Scorpion, also had a reputation for a line with a kink, a questionable temperament.' Josie remembers watching and could hardly credit what they were seeing. 'It was unbelievable, the fact he got up was a miracle. You could see Nico trying so hard to get him to go straight and he just couldn't because Might Bite was stronger than him. When he saw the loose horse he decided to go on. It was amazing, extraordinary; stopping, stopping, stopping, then galloping on.'

She goes on, 'I think that's when the racing public really loved him for the first time and took him to their hearts; they saw this extraordinary display of character. You could see his thought process: I've finished, I've jumped all the fences, I'll go to the stable now … Oh my GOD another horse is coming, I'd better get on. It was very special.'

Gemma Pearson, vet and equine behaviour specialist says, 'This is really common. Horses head back to where they feel safe. It is the same when riders come off eventing, the horses usually try to head back to the stables. This can be a nightmare as they skip over the tape and head back at speed through crowds of people, taking the straightest route.'

Aaron says, 'I don't think I've ever shook like that after a race,' and the rest of it was a blur for him. Might Bite already knew his way around Cheltenham. In the Novices' Hurdle in 2015, Aaron remembers, 'He'd pulled in, when he ran over hurdles. It was a roasting hot day, he decided to pull over, stop for an ice cream half way up the straight and had to start again. He had it in the back of his head over fences.'

Might Bite won by a whisker from Whisper (also Nicky's) with Davy Russell. But Might Bite's rules of engagement had again been ignored as Nicky says, 'My only conclusion was, when Daryl gave him a smack between the last two fences in the Feltham [the race was renamed the Kauto Star Novices' Chase], he fell, it was the last thing he needed, he was winning by miles. He'd led all the way in the RSA and Nico gave him a smack – just one – with Daryl he fell and with Nico he turned right.' The horse could hardly make it clearer.

Come the Grade One Mildmay Novices' Chase at Aintree, his message had been received. Nicky remembers, 'I said to Nico, "Whatever you do, I don't care how well or how badly you're going, don't hit him before the last fence." We had it all planned. Minty was going to stand half way up the run-in with a big mac open to stop him running out. We knew he'd work towards running towards home. At Cheltenham he turned right, where they think they're going back: I've not got to go up that hill?? My own decision was by hitting him, he resented it, that was it, his brain went into meltdown, and he didn't like it and we decided not to.'

Nico remembers his instructions were simple: 'Never pick up your stick before you've jumped the last, so I wasn't allowed to do anything more than hands and heels, to coax him and work with him. That's what it was, work with him, rather than trying to force anything. If he didn't want to do it, he wasn't going to do it.'

Might Bite had finally got people doing as he wished, and not doings things he didn't wish. He pushed Whisper into second again at Aintree, and was free to go on and express himself, and so he did, winning the Intermediate Chase at Sandown, and the Grade One King George Chase at Kempton where he pushed Double Shuffle to second, Tea for Two to third, and Thistlecrack into fourth, before his tilt at the Gold Cup.

By now, the public had taken him to their hearts. The veering right was odd, no doubt, but it was endearing. 'They have to have a character to be loveable and the public decided he was lovable. And that's that. He was lovely at home, and the most beautiful horse, and not quirky,' Nicky says. He wasn't the only thoroughbred with a soupçon of eccentricity by a long chalk. Another much-loved maverick Mad Moose, trained by Nigel Twiston-Davies, refused to use certain gallops, learned to give work days a miss altogether, and often – but not always – refused to race. He was talented enough to have once chased home Sprinter Sacre in 2013; he started, was overtaken by the entire field, then changed his mind as, according to one of his loyal owners Dave Arthur, 'Sprinter Sacre galloped majestically up the straight, Moose decided to start running on, past very decent chasers, and finished second to Sprinter. It was magnificent.' At the Tingle Creek, he started but pulled himself up before the first and sauntered back to delighted crowds cooing 'Mooooooooose', as unrepentant as a pony being eliminated in a gymkhana. Exercising his innate right not to do anything he didn't want to do once too often, he was finally banned in 2014, and advised his fans on social media that his owners were 'going to find something more suited to my unique talents'.

* * *

Back to Cheltenham for the race of races and Might Bite's Gold Cup battle with Native River. Nico remembers, 'It felt like a match race; riding it felt like me and Richard Johnson riding against each other and from our perspective, that's what it was. Turning in, I thought I had him, absolutely, we went to jump the last and we hit a patch of really mucky ground, and I knew it was all over as far as I was concerned. I could have been beaten 20 lengths; I can't believe I wasn't beaten that far. My memory tells me I got beaten a long, long way because I was so deflated. They keep a really nice strip of fresh ground for the Gold Cup and it had been particularly wet and that strip was maybe two horses' widths wide, so myself and Native River were on that fresh strip but after the last that was completely gone. Coming up the hill, the bit where everyone crosses over to get to the two-and-a-half-furlong start, once you hit that it's like going from driving on tarmac to a pot-holed road. It wasn't until I got back to the weighing room that I thought he'd run an absolute blinder, I can't be too disheartened.'

Josie remembers the thrill of it: 'It was so exciting, neck-and-neck the whole way round. I thought coming over the last, he's going to do it, we all thought that. We wanted it for him, and for us and for Nicky. His two other horses had won the Champion Hurdle and the Champion Chase and until Henry de Bromhead, nobody had done the three. Might Bite was the third part of it.' (Buveur d'Air and Barry Geraghty had won the Champion Hurdle by a neck from Melon, and Altior and Nico had beaten Min by seven lengths in the Champion Chase.)

It was an especially tough Gold Cup, Josie remembers, 'He was really battling and I still think if the ground was good … Might Bite never went in the mud, he wasn't a mud lark, he liked good ground. He didn't have very big feet and couldn't get through the mud.' Four pulled up and two fell, out of the 15 runners.

She always knew how intelligent the horse was, how observant, and she's quite sure he knew he hadn't won. 'I always thought he knew he was beaten in the Gold Cup,' she says, 'usually after his races he was excited, but after that he was not just exhausted, he also felt he'd been beaten.'

Do horses know if they have won or lost? Professor Jane Williams says, 'I don't know if they have the cognisant reasoning we do; the horse's brain is not developed in the same way as ours.' Even if they aren't aware of the specific winning and losing nature of a race, she says, 'If they are coming back to the winner's enclosure, with the excitement, atmosphere, the crowd, the energy, being praised, I'd expect the horse to pick up and show behavioural cues on the back of it. It's us driving the behaviour.'

Equine behaviourist Gemma Pearson is clear: 'Horses have no concept of winning or losing. They also would not understand the concept of a finishing line. However, they will associate the winning post with the roar from the crowd, the extra pressure from the jockey and the other horses. I think through training and habit formation, some horses learn to try and get in front of other horses at this point. I don't think they "know" if they did win or not, but they are phenomenal at making associations with the rider's emotions, which probably explains why the riders perceive they react differently if they win or lose.'

Whatever Might Bite picked up after his gruelling Gold Cup, Aaron thinks the race overwhelmed him. He says, 'I don't know what that Gold Cup does to horses, but there are war wounds left on them after it. Running over three miles, in a top-class race, there's no hiding place. It's the cream of the crop, everyone wants to win it, it's the main race of the season, and it left its mark. He was a wicked clever animal, and he thought about it a bit. It bottomed him, and perhaps you're better off ripping the rugs off for the end of the season there and then.' AP McCoy agrees in general, and says, 'It's 100 per cent the toughest race, and it's very hard to get to that level again in a short space of time. Performance in any sport is hard to repeat, there's always a drop in levels after a big event and if I was an owner or trainer, I'd never run a horse after the Gold Cup. You train them for the pinnacle, and you should start again the next year, and head toward the pinnacle again.'

Might Bite had a tough race, but he was never a horse that liked to go by the book. He had one more great run in him and duly arrived in Aintree for his next. Nico says when he was on his game, it was 'like riding a piece of perfect poetry. He ran his best race after the gruelling Gold Cup against Native River, when he went to the Aintree Bowl. We'd worked him the week after, I thought he's feeling really good.' Come the race, Nico remembers he was 'foot perfect, a joy to ride – he was fantastic when he was on his game and he had his own idea of things'. When Josie looks back now, she says, 'It was his last win, it was like he said, "I'll do one more, then I don't want to do it anymore." He lost the taste and nobody will ever quite know why.'

Something was becoming obvious to all even if it wasn't obvious what that something was. Did he lose the taste, a shift that only makes itself known at the racecourse? Possibly, says Nico, 'but not after the Gold Cup'. He says this was a horse that 'did it his way. I wouldn't say he was quirky, when he came down to it, he did put it all in and left everything out on the track. To go from a standing start by the Arkle bar to get up to racing pace and finish the way he did you have to put it all in. They don't go on forever, they're not machines, running in those champion races, there comes a time.'

Aaron noticed he'd lost a certain *joie de vivre*. He describes it as his 'sassiness, the fire in his belly' and that 'he'd get clever, sitting behind the bridle, he wouldn't take you where you wanted to be like the early days and the enthusiasm'. Corky remembers, 'He was a lovely, honest, big horse and he went off it, he had a hard race in the Gold Cup. You can try and get them back but he was never the same, and you have to retire them, if you try again and they've fallen out of love.'

After Aintree, he had a few disappointing runs that baffled Nicky and the team, including being pulled up in the 2019 Gold Cup, and they couldn't know it then, but he didn't win another race. Nicky despatched him for a thorough MOT with equine sports medicine specialist Kate Allen at Bristol University. She says she loved working for Nicky; they'd have a call, discussing the background and his impressions then he'd leave her alone to do her thing, then chat again afterwards. Her first impressions: 'He's so good-looking! He was a really impressive quality horse, he looked really well, as all Nicky's horses did, I could always pick them out,' she says. 'He was gorgeous, I liked him, he was always very easy, though his name made a few people think, riiiiight.'

She kept him for three days of tests and, was so taken by how observant he was that she noted it in her report (which she hadn't ever recorded for any other horses). 'Going on the treadmill is a fairly unusual experience, if they've never done it before,' she says, 'and when they're on, for safety reasons, we have quite a lot of handlers around the horse. Might Bite was very, very aware of where everybody was, and if they moved. It's not something we'd normally pick up on and certainly wouldn't comment on it. No idea what to make of it, what it means, whether it translates in any way to how he trains or races but he was acutely aware of where everyone was and what they were doing. He was keeping an eye out.'

The 'something' that the Gold Cup takes out of a horse is indefinable. Kate says, 'I don't know what that is, it's that willingness to win isn't it? It's not a veterinary thing, it's intangible, it's very difficult to define or describe but athletes have it as well – how hard are you prepared to push yourself to get to the line first?' She's heard plenty of trainers and jockeys say after a hard race that the horse can't give that again. She wonders, if horses push themselves very hard and it's painful and they didn't like the experience, they might not push themselves in that way again. 'Perhaps they're smarter than we give them credit for; if it's not comfortable some do [push themselves] and some don't and prefer to save themselves a bit.'

None of Kate's tests could show her, unequivocally, what had happened. She found a couple of tiny things, such as very mild lameness that Nicky's vet was already monitoring and managing, and it hadn't changed over the year and was so subtle that galloping didn't affect it, and it hadn't altered from when he was winning to not winning, so it wasn't that. None of her findings, together or separately gave her any confidence that they were the reason and if addressed would solve the mystery.

There was one big positive, which was his cardiac response to exercise. 'His heart rate at different points of exercise was incredible, I thought, wow, he's an amazing athlete. You could see his capability was incredible; he was, from the cardio-vascular point of view, genetically gifted, very impressive.'

Kate concluded after her time with this most glamorous of horses: 'Sometimes as a vet you feel confident you've identified what it is, which is an explanation and sometimes you don't. We knew we'd found A, B and C but didn't have any confidence that they were truly the explanation.' And that in itself would have to be the answer. 'If you can find an explanation, great, you can do something, but not finding the explanation gives Nicky reassurance that they've done everything they possibly can to make sure the horse is well and in optimal health.'

After five years of unexpected highs, his owners agreed, he was ready to retire. Josie says simply, 'They could never find anything wrong; his heart wasn't in it anymore and he never really showed his brilliance again.' One of the many surprises he'd given was the way he endeared himself to the public. Josie says, 'It was lovely that other people loved him, lovely to share the love and be a part of something other people love.'

'He'd been in some battles by then, and his heart wasn't quite there,' Nicky says. 'Enough was enough, he was soft, gorgeous, the best jumper you'll see when he could. He had three disappointing races, and his owners wanted to pack up before I did.'

Kate sympathises, 'Trainers have to find the right point: not too soon and not too late,' and without an explicit explanation, his taste for it could have returned. She says, 'The will is unmeasurable but they have to have it.'

The time had come. Aaron was sad to see him go, but glad he could have a second chance. 'You want them to have a happy life afterwards, there's nothing worse than a good horse coming to the end of their career and not being able to live life as a horse again. They've been in big school from the moment they've got their saddles on.' He remembers Might Bite had 'lots of character, he was a presence. He'd tuck himself up, and show himself off, he was always chomping on the bit, when you walked around the paddock, you'd hear people saying, "Wow look at him." He was incredible-looking, I was so proud of him.'

* * *

Might Bite spent his summer holidays with the Vigors family at their stud farm and he wasn't odd at all. Tracy says, 'They know when they're being let down, and he's never bitten anyone here. They know their environment.' He stayed out night and day, no headcollar so no one would know it was him, being fed twice a day, checked three times daily and loving it. 'Some don't cope with it,' Tracy says, 'some love routine, and their stable, and know the horses all around,' but some take to R&R, lying in the field, 'with their heads on each other's bums, or under each other's tails'.

She says it's a pleasure to watch them all being horses, growing their coats, getting well fed if they've had a hard season, and that it doesn't take long for them to wind right down. 'In training,' Tracy says, 'their time is not their own, and it can be frenzied, even after exercise with people past the door.' Nicky keeps an eye on them, still. 'He wants the best for his horses,' Tracy says, 'he can see when one needs something extra. When Altior and Shishkin were on box rest, he'd come and put his arms round them. He loves them, and he comes anytime in the summer, once a week, with Sophie and wanders the paddocks with a sheet, and he writes notes on all of them, with timescales for them all, when he wants them in, which one needs an extra month. He's a real horseman.'

* * *

For a horse that enjoyed creating drama on the racecourse, it's fitting that he has now taken up residency with Charles Barnett, himself no stranger to theatrics at the races. A former amateur jockey, who went on to be managing director of Aintree and chief executive of Ascot, his first year in Liverpool was 1993. It was the year that the Grand National was declared void after two false starts. Charlie remembers the day well: 'It was cold, which blew the tape for the start towards the horses,' and there were demos at the first fence. Nicky was at the start, walking with Richard Dunwoody, who was riding 16/1 Wont Be Gone Long for Robert Waley-Cohen ('he was probably staying with me, he's a very old friend,' says Charles). For the second false start, one of the horses had his head over the tape, which was also wrapped around Richard's neck, and every time a horse trod on it, it yanked him. Now, Charles sees it all as part of 'Aintree's rich tapestry, lots of strange and wonderful things happened, it doesn't distract from the importance of the race.'

He has nothing but praise for his new family member. 'Might Bite is having a nice retirement, I hope. He's extremely well and enjoying life. He's very friendly, very easy to deal with, always quite pleased to get his food.'

He's still ridden, Charlie says, 'He's charming, he hasn't been anything other than a gentleman. He's a gorgeous ride; beautifully balanced, he looks magnificent, a different class.' And still, 'incredibly good-looking. A typical man, my wife would say: he kind of thinks he might be top dog. He likes his friends, gets on with them in the field every day. He likes to roll – a lot – and he's precious.'

He still likes doing things his own way, 'he's pretty independent, very much his own person, not necessarily very close to the others,' as Charles says. He's safe enough for his children to ride, and 'he's pretty good at talking to my grandchildren too. If I'm riding, and leading him and riding another, he'll try and bite the other horse's neck or my leg but it's not vicious.' Might Bite indeed.

CONSTITUTION HILL

The horse of extremes; one half electrifying talent, the other zoned-out serenity

CONSTITUTION HILL'S victory in the 2023 Festival's Champion Hurdle was agony for his owner Michael Buckley. As he accompanied the horse back to his now familiar place in the winner's enclosure, 'I found myself wrestling with a huge man who put his arms round me trying to tell how wonderful it was. I'd had an accident on Monday morning, and I didn't know till after the Festival that I'd fractured my shoulder. So, everyone was patting me on the back, saying well done, and it hurt like hell.'

For everyone else, it was heavenly. It was the opening day, Tuesday, 14 March, and at around 3.15pm the parade ring was as crowded as a rush-hour platform; a sense of excitement hung in the air. Six horses for the Grade One Champion Hurdle were prowling the ring with one more to come. Constitution Hill was still getting dressed in the pre-parade ring (when Nicky had checked on him earlier that day, he'd reported to Michael that he was fast asleep). Here, now, he wasn't fidgeting, biting the bit, nodding his head, or swivelling his ears. Like crew triple-checking the ropes before launching a yacht, Nicky adjusted the hundreds of straps and buckles that keep the saddle where it should be and the horse was completely unbothered. A select crowd stood in a half circle around him, at a discreet distance, talking softly, but all the time with one eye watching him. This gleaming bay with a small white star, looked back with no more than mild curiosity.

When he loped into the parade ring for a single circuit, Alice Plunkett, ITV racing presenter, noticed his 'zen-like' quality and says, 'I was struck by his eye, his amazing big, brown, kind eye. He's so centred and so solid in himself, no insecurity in any way, no anxiety, nothing that worries him. I was so taken with his demeanour, the way he handles himself, such extraordinary calm and confidence.'

Nicky, Nico de Boinville and Michael had talked it all through and through, everyone's opinion had been aired, the plan of action agreed. 'Michael knows how to read a race very well,' Nico says, and they'd decided he should 'start a bit wider, you never know what the Irish lads are going to do, box you in, or play a tactical game, so I wanted to start wide and slot in. If you get penned in on the rails it can be very hard to get out of that position.'

In the last seconds before the jockey was boosted into the saddle, the pressure shifted. Nico says, 'It's harder for the guv'nor and Michael Buckley because at that point, it's not in their control, it's then I take over and it's all up to me now.' A few last words, racing goggles on, down the horse walk, and a canter to the start.

Constitution Hill was the 4/11 favourite. He'd won all five of his previous starts under Rules. The previous year, he'd won the Festival's Novices' Hurdle by 22 lengths from his mighty stablemate Jonbon and set a course record. On his last outings before this race, he'd trounced another stablemate Epatante, once by 12 lengths in the Fighting Fifth at Newcastle, then again by 17 lengths in the Christmas Hurdle at Kempton. He'd gone straight to the top, on the bridle, and stayed there.

Flag start, they're off, Nico and the Hill out to the side, a little wide, the crowd could see every thrumming step as they tracked the leader. He crossed the hurdles like an arrow: long, low, whip-crack quick. They swung to the third last, he leapt into the lead at the second last. His only competition was the seriously good State Man with Paul Townend but they were never going to catch him. And then, a *huge* leap over the last hurdle, Nico says, 'I knew coming to it, ten strides out, we weren't going to meet it right, I didn't for the life of me think he was going to do that! Luckily, we were rolling forward and we had enough momentum that he could get up and out the other side.' Jockey Patrick Mullins was standing at the last and later told Michael he saw the horse lift his front legs two inches *while he was in the air* to make sure he cleared the hurdle. Constitution Hill accelerated around the final turn, powered to four or five lengths clear for his motionless jockey, as they left the field in his wake. The sun caught his quarters, his tail streamed behind him, his mane lifted in the wind, he was flying, storming the hill, untouchable, magnificent, other.

He passed the post, first by what seemed to be a comfortable, almost chosen, nine lengths and it was all over in about four minutes. The crowd must be getting used to not seeing another horse in shot at the line. It was Nicky's ninth Champion Hurdle and that rarest of races, a no-contest thriller. Nico says, 'I went into the day thinking that I must try and enjoy today, days like this are why we're doing what we do, it's not often you get to ride a horse like him, I really tried to enjoy it, every single moment. I loved the race; it was great fun to ride and it couldn't have gone any better.'

Michael remembers before the race, 'I was shaky, I'd invested nervous energy without realising it,' and after, 'It was a struggle to get off the stand, we walked through the tunnel and everyone was cheering. It was really touching; I couldn't believe the huge crowd gathered round us as we walked from the track to the paddock.' Michael Dickinson (who trained the first five home in the 1983

Gold Cup) told him his horse was the best horse in the air he'd ever seen in his life, the best horse he'd seen since Arkle (who won three consecutive Gold Cups at the Festival in 1964-66, among countless other prizes and was so exceptional a new, separate handicapping system was introduced when he ran).

As the horse sauntered back to the winner's enclosure, led by his groom Jaydon Lee, he was so relaxed, Nico remembers, 'He tripped over, as we came off the walkway, he had a little trip!' What he describes as 'a magical, electric atmosphere' made no impression on the horse. He was barely blowing, had hardly broken sweat, remained unfazed by the people rushing to touch his neck and breathe the same air. He was the parade ring's pied piper and he didn't flinch. You'd call it grace under pressure but he hadn't been under any. The expectations are immense, and for Michael, it's a stress that he can handle, as he says, 'If you're the best, you get a lot of pressure to, say, retain the title, but it's only because you're having a great life. I love it, it's fantastic, I'm in awe of the horse and very proud of him.'

This horse is brilliant.

* * *

Nicky's first take on Constitution Hill couldn't have been more different. He was so s-l-o-w when he arrived at Seven Barrows, he caused traffic queues in the covered school. 'He starts at the back, two laps later he's in front, all the others have caught him up. Then we trot, the same thing happens, he just plods around in his own time.' He called Barry Geraghty, who had co-owned the horse for three years with Warren Ewing and said, 'This horse is a yak!' In response, Barry sent pictures of his daughter sitting on the horse as he lay in his box. 'That doesn't prove he's good,' Nicky said, 'it proves his temperament, which I don't doubt, but I need a racehorse and he belongs in the Pony Club!' 'Keep the faith,' Barry assured him. Trog, trog, trog went the Hill.

When Barry had brought the horse to the sales, Minty already knew of him, (Minty knows of all the horses) but as this exceptional bloodstock agent with the unerring eye and decades of experience at the very highest level remembers, 'to put it nicely he did not look at his best, I couldn't believe a horse could come to the sales looking so weak. I was not amused.' He felt so strongly about it that he told Nicky that he couldn't buy him. The horse had been much talked-up by Barry and Warren, and Michael remembers a couple of casual, infrequent conversations he'd had with Barry about this horse, over many months, with no view to buy.

The Hill was suffering from an adverse reaction to antibiotics but Barry always believed in him, and Nicky always had confidence in Barry. Michael did too, though he wasn't at the sales and asked Nicky to call him with news. The horse looked 'shocking'. Oh well, there we go, thought Michael. Nicky's second impression: worse than he thought, he looked terrible. What to do, wondered Michael and despite everything, decided to buy him, as the only bidder, for £120,000.

When he won the Supreme Novices' Hurdle at the Festival the following March, Michael remembers, 'At least four to six people said, "I looked at him, and couldn't have bought him." After the third one, I said, "What are you trying to tell me – I'm an idiot? I already know that." It was just a punt, a piece of luck, and nothing more.'

* * *

Michael has had horses in training with Nicky for many decades and remembers 'early on, he used the expression about one that I had with him, "he's a really nice person". It surprised me that he refers to horses like that, he really does think of them in that way. The depth to which he feels for these horses might surprise people.'

Unfortunately, Michael's experience as an owner started well. 'The first horse I ever owned won a race. That was a disaster, because then I was hooked. I worked out quite quickly, the most important decision you can make if you're owning horses, is who you choose as a trainer. Obviously, you're going to choose someone who can produce a horse to win a race, but more important is someone with whom you can get through the bad days.'

Anyone can celebrate a win, and enjoy the good times, but 'it's when you have a rough day, and everything goes wrong, it's important to be with someone who deals with that well, someone you feel compatible with, to understand the misfortune. Suddenly you don't have a horse, it's heartbreaking.' After so many years, it's never occurred to Michael to send his horses anywhere else. 'We're so different,' he says, 'I've got so many things I'm interested in away from horses, he's consumed by it, but we get on well, he's nice, kind, decent and I'm very fond of him.'

He adds Nicky is 'utterly, absurdly superstitious; if he sees a magpie, and he's driving to the races, he goes about 40 miles to find a tunnel with a train running over it'. When he advised Michael that he couldn't come to the races in a green tie, he remembers, 'I looked at the tweedy country folk in green suits and thought, what's he on about?' That said, Michael was wearing a red tie with white horses and hearts when his beloved Finian's Rainbow won the Champion Chase in 2012, and has worn it every time one of his horses has run since, and always will.

* * *

Constitution Hill was brought into rude health at the Vigorses' stud, where Nicky's horses spend their summer holidays, and once he began his training, Nicky told Minty, 'You were right, this horse is *so slow*.' Increasingly frustrated, one morning he asked his jockey James Bowen to shake the reins, see what he's got. Three horses set off at the bottom of the gallops, due to arrive three abreast, and only one appeared, lobbing up the hill, miles ahead.

Crikey, thought Nicky, is that who I think it is?

'What?' an unconcerned Constitution Hill might have asked when he saw the wide eyes and dropped jaws.

'Oh dear,' Nicky was back on the phone to Minty, 'I think we're wrong, he's just taken off up the gallops and I've never seen anything like it.' Pony Club's loss, National Hunt's gain.

Nico says his 'instant turn of foot is pretty staggering, and you wouldn't have a clue until you do that faster work'. The horse prefers to live quietly away from the hustle and bustle, just as Sprinter Sacre did before him, and while he is famously at ease, he's no pushover; there is a streak of steel. Nico says, 'It's there, just lurking under the surface. When he's fresh and well, you can't rest on your laurels, and think he's just going to bumble in back home. He can try it on, you have to be careful, or you'll be on the floor before you know it. His lad who rides him every day says you need your wits about you when he's fresh.'

He's exceptional in two ways. One is his temperament, and the other is his athleticism. His proud breeder Sally Noott is now delighted when people who vaguely know she's involved in racing ask her if she has any runners at Cheltenham. 'No,' she says, without a trace of sadness … 'I did breed Constitution Hill though.'

The earliest stages of development matter. Sally thinks the key to his relaxed ways could be that when his dam, Queen of the Stage, returned to her, having given birth at a nearby stud, she had an injury to her back leg. Sally remembers, 'She stopped in for two or three weeks, she couldn't go out in case she got an infection. The foal was in for the same time, so he was handled at an early stage. He was never any trouble.'

Minty agrees that 'handling the stock as youngsters is a big plus'. Constitution Hill's sire Blue Bresil is known as a 'slow breeder', in that he 'only' covers one or two mares a day, so maybe he passed a certain composure down the line.

When this little foal went to live with Barry Geraghty, he remembers, 'He was literally at my back door for three years and he was the family pet.' He was ridden by Barry's daughters Siofra (then 15), Órla (then 9) and his son Rian who was just five, (whether lying in his box or being trit-trotted round the school), and led out of the field and off the horse-walker by them. 'He wasn't completely docile and dopey, but he had good energy, he was good fun, in a playful way, and a really kind individual.' From a pet to the podium at Cheltenham, it's a family affair. Barry remembers when the horse won the Supreme, Nicky said to him, "Your family is our family and our family is your family." It is, he says, 'dreamland stuff'.

Minty says, 'The horse doesn't have a care in the world, his big forte is his temperament, I'm in awe of him. He's an extraordinary horse, he switches on, does his job and comes back as if nothing's happened. He's a one-off.' Michael says, 'It's bizarre, I can't believe people picked up on him so fast, he's not the one you'd pick out in a line-up, with a huge physique or black coat, but he gets the job done, he's very calm about it, he deals with the adulation, gets on with life.' The horse is an undisputed star, but as Michael says, 'he doesn't take many curtain calls'.

And then, there is the athleticism which is his own star-power. 'He doesn't really have the charisma,' Nicky, always taken by the glamour, admits, 'He tells his own story by pure brilliance and being so wonderfully laid back. Racing doesn't get him very excited, which doesn't make him very exciting. The beauty of it is his head, it's half the reason for his brilliance.'

'His jumping is not flamboyant, it's a bit brutal, it reminds you of a paid assassin,' says ITV commentator Richard Hoiles. 'He gets on with the hit, does it, picks up his bags and goes home – no patting himself on the back for the head-shot from 200 yards. He has obvious class, even people who don't follow racing can see it; it's like Messi playing football. Even at Cheltenham, he stands out as a bit different, it looks to come more easily to him, more naturally, without any effort before or after. He isn't physically over-impressive, you wouldn't pick him out, he looks mortal, not a demigod, just better.'

Steve Smith-Eccles, no stranger to winning Champion Hurdles, says his racing style reminds him of the mighty See You Then. Corky goes further, saying, 'He's better than See You Then, he's faster, he quickens in the last three furlongs. He's a machine. He could win four Champion Hurdles and have one more season.' AP McCoy says, 'He's a wonderful horse. Brilliance can happen once or twice, greatness is longevity. Next year we'll see a little more, if he's got the potential. The longer he remains unbeaten the closer he gets to greatness.'

The public has taken him to their hearts, so much so that Michael says, 'He's somewhat ceased to be mine. He doesn't belong to me; the public is nice enough to lease him back to me to run in my colours.' He's caught people's imagination, from Michael's 'pals in Ireland who've been knocking around the horse world a long time, and they all love him,' to strangers stopping him in the street, to the dozens he watched crowd the pre-parade at Newcastle before winning the Fighting Fifth ('when he came in, they were shouting "Nico Nico Nico" around the winner's enclosure') to a cab driver who asked for a tip. 'Of course, cash or card?' Michael said. 'No,' the cabbie replied, 'a racing tip, I know who you are.'

Constitution Hill finished with another easy-looking win at Aintree, though as Nicky always points out, there is no such thing at this level. Effortless rarely is. When he paraded at Sandown for jump racing's send off, the loudspeakers, crowds, racing and crackling excitement had no effect on him at all. Jaydon brought him in to the middle of the parade ring, and he grazed as if alone and at peace in a meadow. 'At one point, his leg buckled and I thought he was going to roll,' Michael remembers, 'he's so relaxed, he's consistent that way. Nicky said he's the only horse on the planet you could do this with in the paddock.' (For comparison, Vicky Roberts paraded Sprinter Sacre at Sandown in 2022, six years after he had retired, and ten years on from his thrilling Tingle Creek win. He was explosive in the ring, and airborne as he led the runners onto the course. He was still fizzing three days later, and it took the best part of a week for him to get his appetite back. A hot breakfast eventually did the trick.)

So, what now? In a box two days after that Champion Hurdle, flat trainer par excellence John Gosden asked Nicky exactly that. He replied, 'We'll probably find out somewhere along the line how far he stays and we'll see … we might have a look at the Gold Cup.' 'That would be great, to see him over three-and-a-quarter miles,' enthused John. Nicky replied, 'No, not Cheltenham, I mean the Ascot Gold Cup.' 'You wouldn't dare!' 'Don't try me.' This is a horse so special that Nicky needs to specify which Gold Cup he's talking about, the flat or the jumps. He's literally a horse for all seasons.

There is such a thing as chemistry, and timing and sorcery and Alice Plunkett says that this horse is Nicky's Frankel, because 'the right horse met the right trainer at the right time'.

Nicky is the best trainer of the best horses, he's been at the top of his game for 40 years. Nicky responds, 'Honestly he is the ABC of training racehorses. He's so straightforward it's not true. The only thing that's complicated my life is that he's so much better than anyone else. Nothing else can go with him.'

After his 2023 summer holidays, his career will be mapped out, he will school over fences and then Nicky says, 'We'll see and sit down and discuss it. He could win the Champion Hurdle, go novice chasing … if he jumps like a hurdler he'll stay hurdling. We'll see, *au naturel*, if he's got the brain. He'll jump five fences on his own, we'll look to give one a bit of a nudge, he'll find out these are quite solid and he'll tell us very quickly.' No pressure, beautiful bay superstar, but it took Altior just two goes to work it out.

Michael says, 'My instinct is that he'll probably stay hurdling next season.' He's heard all the conjecture and says, 'It's entirely my fault, I said wouldn't it be fun to do a Dawn Run, to win a Gold Cup as well as a Champion Hurdle.' Nico's looking forward to the discussions either way. 'I've been at Seven Barrows so long, I feel I can speak freely and I do, sometimes I'm told that's a load of rubbish and sometimes that's a good idea but it's an open dialogue, and honest talk.'

Minty has no doubts about the future. He says, 'Whatever he does, he'll be brilliant. He's such a neat jumper, exceptionally correct and quick, and he'll be the same over fences. He looks after himself, which helps him to stay sound.' Nico agrees that the only question is his staying power: 'If he doesn't have the stamina to win a Gold Cup there's little point going over fences.' Even for a horse that is blatantly brilliant, it's never easy, as Nicky adds, 'It's tough, and it's great if you win two Champion Hurdles, three is an absolute miracle, and you've kept the horse sane and sound.'

The buck stops with Nicky; it's a permanent houseguest at Seven Barrows. There'll be no shortage of people who know exactly what he should do, and shouldn't, and should but won't, and when, and how. This is the horse to watch, this is the horse to beat.

Nicky's been here before. 'If you've got those horses you live with the pressure of it. Do you want it or don't you want it? We'd been through three weeks of hell getting to Cheltenham. Which would you have: the pressure of what it is and finish up with the pot of gold or someone else having the horse and us not having to worry? That's what it's all about and that's why we do it.'

A final word on the Hill. Nicky says, 'I hate talking about where we're going to go next year. He's got to sail the Atlantic, swim the Channel, cross a desert without water, and climb Mount Everest, and then he gets to Cheltenham. How many can do all of that?'

We'll find out.